The Wilder Heart of Florida

THE WILDER HEART
of FLORIDA

More Writers Inspired by Florida Nature

Edited by Jack E. Davis and Leslie K. Poole

Foreword by Temperince Morgan

UNIVERSITY OF FLORIDA PRESS
Gainesville

Frontis: "Lamplighter at Night on the Santa Fe," by Margaret Ross Tolbert

Copyright 2021 by Jack E. Davis and Leslie K. Poole
Published in the United States of America. Printed on acid-free paper.

26 25 24 23 22 21   6 5 4 3 2 1

Library of Congress Control Number: 2020938176
ISBN 978-1-68340-163-6

University of Florida Press
2046 NE Waldo Road
Suite 2100
Gainesville, FL 32609
http://upress.ufl.edu

UF PRESS

UNIVERSITY
OF FLORIDA

This book is dedicated to the memory
of Nathaniel "Nat" Pryor Reed (1933–2018),
whose heart was filled with love for wildlife
and natural beauty, which sustained his lifelong work
to save Florida's wild places for future generations.

Contents

Foreword

In Florida, nature isn't out there—it's right here. From the moment you step outside, there's no escaping the cloying, relentless heat and shirt-soaking humidity. Our days are often defined by mercurial weather. Torrential downpours descend in full daylight on what was moments before a cloudless day. Even when we're safe at home, we wage war with palmetto bugs, lizards, and even the occasional snake that tries to creep its way in.

Yet, despite all the challenges, anyone who has spent time here can't help but fall under the spell of our weird, wild state. When the weather is cooler, we hike through cypress swamps, hammocks, marshes, and longleaf pine forests. At our state parks, such as Paynes Prairie, American bison roam alongside wild Spanish horses and alligators. And no matter where you find yourself in Florida, you are no more than a short day trip from a beautiful beach or one of our thousand crystal-clear freshwater springs—some of the most serene and stunning places in the world.

Perhaps it's no surprise, then, that Florida's freshwaters always fascinated me growing up here. My family would visit Silver Glen Springs, Juniper Springs, and Salt Springs in the sprawling Ocala National Forest. We'd dive into the 72-degree water and explore what felt like a natural aquarium—a place where swimming around a bend was an adventure that could reveal manatees, turtles, otters, or even a sunbathing gator. Those childhood trips got me hooked on nature. As I got older, the Suwannee River provided the backdrop for some of my defining moments. It's where I spent my summers at camp learning to canoe, swim, and identify bird species, and where I later taught younger campers to do the same. During college, I picnicked along the Suwannee's sandy banks with the person who would one day become my husband. We would take our friends there—many of whom had never been—to camp and kayak down the river and show them just how beautiful Florida can be.

There is no me without growing up here. I know how special Florida is, and I know just how much we stand to lose. Today, Florida's story is changing. As our population continues to grow by over 300,000 people each year, our natural resources face extraordinary pressure to provide for more people, slowly inching out wildlife and constraining our natural beauty.

The first edition of *The Wild Heart of Florida*, which inspired this book, included some of Florida's most well-known writers sharing their affection for the state and their commitment to restoring and conserving its wild spaces. This current volume is a look at Florida twenty years later. In these pages you'll see the ways our state continues to face many of the same issues we faced then. Today, more land has been lost to development, but thanks to the tireless work of conservationists many environmentally precious lands have been protected as well. The Florida landscape is still at risk, and one way we can help change the future of our state is by keeping the conversation going. What does it mean to live in a place that is always in flux? Why is Florida worth protecting? What will Florida look like twenty years from now? And most importantly, how can we protect Florida's beloved wild spaces for the next generation? By telling stories of what makes Florida unique, we can understand more clearly what we stand to lose, and push for more people to protect what we all so dearly love.

I'm proud to be leading the Florida Chapter of The Nature Conservancy, working to protect Florida's wild places for people and for nature. Across Florida we've protected more than 1.2 million acres of vulnerable lands and waters.

Even on issues where there seems to be little hope, such as confronting climate change, we continue to push forward solutions that we think will work. In 2017, we worked with partners to foster bipartisan support for clean energy through a pro-solar ballot measure—which won with more than 70 percent of the vote.

The Conservancy has worked in Florida for over fifty-five years. We know Florida's diversity of landscapes and people intimately, as our teams of conservation practitioners live and work across the entire state. Our state faces many threats, including the looming perils of climate change. It can be easy to slip into pessimism, but I really do feel hopeful about our future. I think of advocates like Greta Thunberg and others like her—young people with a level of passion and conviction that can change hearts and minds. In 2018, Greta's protest in front of the Swedish parliament swept the world when she started the School Strike for Climate movement. Her push for action led to a global school strike that included 1.4 million students across 123 countries.

Finally, I have hope because I believe that most people innately understand the profound importance of nature to our lives and our future. Our most pressing challenge is to find ways to connect the dots between hearts and minds. I believe if we tap into that connection, we can find a way to mobilize people to take action and change the future of our world.

Temperince Morgan
Executive Director
The Nature Conservancy in Florida

Introduction

LESLIE K. POOLE AND JACK E. DAVIS

I do not understand how any one can live
without some small place of enchantment to turn to.

Marjorie Kinnan Rawlings, *Cross Creek* (1942)

With the dawn of each day, Floridians awaken to a rapidly diminishing future for the state's unique and glorious natural systems. As the bulldozers rev up, cars enter highways, and construction cranes begin to swing, our wild spaces become more precious and threatened. The loss is not only habitat for flora and fauna, but also reflects a darkening of the state's soul—a place built on the idea of finding Eden, health, and beauty.

What better way to understand and acknowledge the magnitude of such losses than to celebrate our wildest treasures? That is the goal of *The Wilder Heart of Florida*, a compilation of essays and poems—most of them never before published—in which thirty-four essayists describe places and events that spark their love of irreplaceable landscapes and seascapes. The first volume in this series, published in 1999, offered varied views of the state. Twenty years later, a new slate of authors adds to this conversation with old and new memories of how enfolding themselves in nature has enriched their lives.

They carry on the tradition of our country's greatest nature writers. John

Muir inspired the world to cherish the overwhelming splendor of Yosemite National Park, as well as Cedar Key, Florida, where he conceptualized the basis for his conservation ethos. Henry David Thoreau took readers along on treks in the Maine woods and to the shores of Walden Pond where he connected close observations of the wider universe with nature, including ice cut for the market and shipped to southern places, including Florida. In more modern times, Marjory Stoneman Douglas, featured in this collection, taught us how to value the vast Everglades and their biological richness despite the incessant bugs and seemingly monotonous sawgrass expanses that stretch to the horizon.

Writers in this new anthology also take readers with them, whether they are kayaking wilderness streams, seeking birds in coastal marshes, or hiking in piney scrub. Some tell of tangles with alligators and pythons, while others marvel at the beauty of flowing springs and sandy seashores. Others recall childhood adventures and trips that are written indelibly on their memories and hearts. With this affection comes the impetus to protect pristine ecosystems, and to bring back damaged ones.

Floridians largely agree. In 2014, voters, with a 75 percent majority, passed Amendment 1, known as the Florida Water and Land Conservation Amendment. It changed the state constitution to provide substantial funding for acquisition and protection of natural lands that are increasingly at risk. The substantial support from residents may reflect the hard truth that after living here a lifetime, or even just a few years, everyone has witnessed some place of beauty disappearing to the state's perpetual growth.

Two years after the Amendment 1 vote, the *Florida 2070* report, created by the 1000 Friends of Florida, the University of Florida's GeoPlan Center, and the state Department of Agriculture and Consumer Services, predicted that the state's population—estimated at 21.6 million in 2019—will swell to 33.7 million by 2070, while development will consume some five million acres of rural, agricultural, and natural lands. That will amount to a mind-boggling loss of pastures, forests, and wetlands, vital to recharging the Floridan aquifer and moderating the regional climate, to asphalt, strip malls, and cookie-cutter housing, leaving the state at risk of becoming what author Carl Hiaasen has likened to "Newark with palm trees." In the meantime, algae blooms appear more frequently in the state's fresh- and saltwaters, and luxuriant springs that once inspired poets are becoming cloudy, discolored, and dry.

Never before has Florida been in such peril of losing its essence. Yet wisdom in nature persists.

Through various programs since 1990, Florida has preserved some 25 percent of its natural lands, but they need love and tending, while other critical pieces—wildlife corridors, habitat, recharge expanses, flood-abatement areas, storm buffers, filtering zones, natural carbon sinks—are set aside for protection. Of course those areas that are preserved are always at risk of the next development proposal that might seek exceptions, exemptions, and variances to mine, drill, or build.

Attitudes can and have changed. A century ago, politicians were elected on blustering promises to drain the Everglades, considered a major wasteland and hindrance to progress. Today, politicians gain office on promises to repair them in the world's largest ecological fix, now estimated at a cost of more than $30 billion. And we are thinking more and more about this idea of restoration, of fixing ecological problems—which translate invariably into social and economic problems—that both well-intentioned and not-so-well-intentioned human engineering has historically wrought.

The Wilder Heart of Florida hopes to teach and inspire. Authors have donated their writings to this collection, royalties from which will go to The Nature Conservancy's Florida Chapter, a nonprofit, nonpartisan participant in the larger popularly supported effort to preserve Florida's natural places, vital for humans and wildlife alike. We live in a time when extensive and invaluable scientific research can enlarge our understanding of the natural environment. But a story has the capacity to reach beyond the intellectual to touch something within, an instinct or primordial memory, that turns one's attention more acutely to the animating world that gives not just pleasure but life itself. Perhaps the observations, experiences, and emotions shared in this collection of essays will inspire deeper thinking and constructive conversations about consequential issues related to the human condition and Florida nature. The one is inseparable from the other.

PART I

BECKONINGS

Seduction in Key West

SUSAN LILLEY

Back behind the white-lattice cafes with their fragrant garlic
and Key Lime daiquiris, vines that go back centuries
grow wild around the dumpster. Long before
the gay tea dances and Hemingway and smugglers
and rum runners, this string of islands witnessed steel-hearted
pirates and Spaniards seeking gold, Seminoles, and the murderous
Calusas, who executed enemies by tying them
to the green manchineel apple tree and walking
away to let the tree's poison sap eat slowly
through the clothing to the skin,
to the bones underneath.

It's Saturday, and the cruise ship opens its maw
like a great white and expels the tourists onto dizzy
Duval Street. The town is ready for them with conch
fritters, salty edged tequila, clattering shell necklaces,
and a replica of an eye-gouging machine
at the Pirate Torture Museum. Six times a day the guides
at Hemingway's revive old scandals, still tart and delicious
after fifty years. Ghosts must love the old
gossip here in the glimmery aquamarine daylight.
Vacation girls show off new henna tattoos
on ankles and arms and down low on sunburned backs.

No Calusas remain. But the poison apple still grows
on the smallest, wildest keys, flowering and sending forth
seductive green fruit, which most creatures wisely ignore.
Even a tiny Key deer knows better than to stand
under this tree in the rain. But imagine a tourist
who seeks the unspoiled, who might take a canoe
without guide or map, negotiate the floating mangroves
that encircle each island like a guardian net of leaves,
and filled with wonder, walk his camera to the inevitable
clearing where, in a dim circle of a forgotten
world, this lonely tree waits
and spreads its bright green danger.

The Story under the Story

LAUREN GROFF

Say *Florida* and a vision of the state materializes in the air before me. It is the Florida I love in my bones, the path where I run nearly every morning in Gainesville's Paynes Prairie. In the vision it is always late winter, just before dawn, when the night is fading into purple and there's a snap of cold in the air. The fog rises in puffs off the grass and spindly sapling oaks, and the moment the sun appears in full, the light slides from vague plum gleam into a stronger and more clarifying white, so that the wisps are suddenly illuminated from within. Each fillip, in shifting, seems a living thing, or perhaps a once-living thing, a ghost making itself visible; it is true that Florida is the most haunted of states, a place where the membrane between the worlds is tissue-thin. Soon the grasses catch the light, and each blade shines out a radiant gold, demanding to be seen individually, and not in smeared collective of field or tuft that later light elides it into. Slowly in the distance come clear the first flowering trees of the year, the eastern redbuds with their shy pink frills, the Chickasaw plums in white. The birds begin to stir: the red-winged blackbirds with their chucks and shrills, the doves' sweet soft call, the sandhill cranes with their clicks and whirrs. Not long ago, on a run on Paynes Prairie, I stopped to watch an eight-foot alligator, his spine bedecked in clumps of grassy mud and water hyacinths as though he'd donned camouflage, creeping through the shallows. I saw him make his way toward an ibis standing one-legged in the water, glowing like a candle, utterly nonchalant that these were to be his last few moments upon the earth.

This is my own perfect idea of Florida, yet it is only the topmost of the visions I have of this state, which are infinite and often contradictory. Place is never single—it is multiple; we all see the places we love as palimpsests of uncountable layers. Scratch shallowly, and you will find weary daily ideas, which can shift based on very little, blood-sugar dips or an irritation at the empty coffee pot. I have overheard a snide remark in a café, and suddenly the entire state of Florida seemed bleak and loveless. Yet I have also seen an eight-foot rat snake stretched in the sun across my path, his scales gleaming in the midsummer heat like beaten copper, the whole stretch of him beneath the skin a pure and clenching muscle, and the gift of him within the otherwise ordinary day made Florida into a place worthy of the gods. And scratch deeply, you will find the foundational collective myths that have entered us as fact. These are so deeply embedded they are often impossible to shake or shift; these ideas of place are the ones that prove themselves to be as implacable as stone.

At its deepest levels, my own personal Florida has been created out of the words and images of other writers, the love that they bear for this place crystallizing into an understanding that acts as bedrock beneath my momentary perceptions of the state. Writers mediate the difficulties of the world through books, the ones that we read in order to feel as though we are in the company of people who understand us, the ones that we write in order to understand the world. "I've got the map of Florida on my tongue," said the great novelist and folklorist Zora Neale Hurston. If you come to the idea of Florida as an adult, the way I did, you do begin to create your map of the state through words. My first Florida—beyond the childhood visits to Disney World, which is not really Florida, just a mirage projected out of bulldozed citrus groves—came when I was an undergraduate in college, and I thought I was a poet. (Reader, I was not). I found a new and dazzling idea of Florida in Elizabeth Bishop's poem named after the state, in which she says Florida is *The state with the prettiest name/ the state that floats in brackish water/ held together by mangrove roots/ that bear while living oysters in clusters.* This was the first vision I had of Florida beyond the stock-photo ideas of bronzed retirees walking hand-in-hand on white sand beaches, or six-foot Minnie Mouses miming at hotel breakfast buffets. Bishop taught me that there was a better, far more fascinating Florida just beyond my reach.

Still, in 2006, when my husband and I moved to Florida, I felt sad and mismatched. I had been raised in the landscape of upstate New York, with its cold lakes and hills. The geography of a place molds the philosophy of the people who live there, and my natal philosophy—wariness, reticence, intellectualism, coolness—felt wrong in the constant searing sunlight, the humidity, the heat, the insects, the large-sky flatness, the teeming nature of life in the Sunshine State. But I remembered Bishop's lesson and went to the library two blocks from my house and took out all of the books about Florida I could find, dipping and tasting, searching and skimming, until I opened John McPhee's nonfiction book about Florida, *Oranges,* and was sucked in for hours. McPhee made me laugh, he made me think, he made me look closely at this place and see that it is worthy of long, considered, focused interest.

Soon after this, my father-in-law, who had been born in Gainesville, told me that in the 1940s, when he was a hyperactive child of about six or so, his mother took him to the dry goods store, where he would shove his fists as deeply as he could into the barrels of sunflower seeds and oats, contaminating them. One day he heard a deep woman's voice scolding his mother, and when they left the store, the mother let him know that a famous person, a Pulitzer Prize–winning author, had just told her to keep her brat under control. I had read Marjorie Kinnan Rawlings's *The Yearling* as a child, but it left my consciousness swiftly, perhaps because, as I found out when I read it in my late twenties, it isn't a children's book at all, although readers have somehow been manipulated into reading it as one. In fact, *The Yearling* is a gorgeous, slow-moving river of a book about subsistence-level Floridians living at a time before air-conditioning or refrigerators or modern food storage methods—a time when a beloved pet deer who leaps fences and eats a family's garden would certainly sign his own death warrant. As an adult, I found most exquisite the parts of the book where the boy Jody felt an ecstatic joy at the natural world of Florida—the great bear hunt, the dance of the whooping cranes, the flood after the hurricane. During her writing years Rawlings lived on her own orange grove not far from Gainesville, delighting in the backwoods bootleggers and frog giggers and hunters and fishermen she came to know. By the time I looked up from *The Yearling,* I had learned to borrow Rawlings's eyes; it was through her first perceptions and the palpable love with which she beheld the state of Florida that I began to take great delight in the strange and wild natural world all around me.

My interest in literary Florida then became a full-blown fever, and I gulped up everything written about the state that I could find. Chief among my loves is William Bartram, the great Quaker naturalist who came through Florida between 1773 and 1777 and wrote with quivering ecstatic beauty about it. Here he writes, so magnificently, about an alligator: "Behold him rushing forth from the flags and reeds. His enormous body swells. His plaited tail, brandished high, floats upon the lake. The waters like a cataract descend from his opening jaws. Clouds of smoke issue from his dilated nostrils. The earth trembles with his thunder." And I love Peter Matthiessen's *Shadow Country*, the wicked joyous novel about settler days in the Ten Thousand Islands, with its exquisite prose. "In the wake of hurricane," Matthiessen writes on the first page, "the coast lies broken, stunned. Day after day, a brooding wind nags at the mangroves, hurrying the unruly tides that hunt through the flooded islands and dark labyrinthine creeks of the Ten Thousand Islands. Brown spume and matted salt grass, driftwood: a far gray sun picks up dead glints from the windrows of rotted mullet at high water line." I love so many writers: Joy Williams, Harry Crews, a slew of newer writers who teach me how to see this strange place as even stranger than I had believed it to be.

It is important, vital, even, to read stories about the places we share. Our human brains are trained to recognize in the world what we have been primed by narrative to see. Narrative is the deepest and oldest of human tools; narrative is what separates humans from other animals, this ability to organize the past in order to drive future actions. And the writers who are the most sensitive and perceptive about the natural wonders of our state are the very same writers to whom I respond most fully. Through them I learned how to *see* Florida, to discover the words to identify the birds and palms and trees and insects that teem joyously here, to understand the way that each part of the ecology fits into the larger whole, to understand the history of the people here and how we have fit, or misfit, ourselves into the natural world. It is narrative that has given me the way to love Florida, primarily through the writers' own love of the natural environment. Florida's delicate environment is our greatest glory and treasure; the extraordinary variety of our ecologies is the deep, immeasurable wealth of our state. Anyone who has floated on innertubes down the Ichetucknee River and seen an anhinga's dark wings gloriously outstretched in the sunlight to dry; or who has spent a night watching sea turtles being born on Crescent Beach; or who has sat on a dock watching the sun set over the gulf, eating clams, snagged from the water only minutes before and then grilled, with a nice salad and a beautiful glass of Sancerre, can attest to this.

Yet our ecological zones—so diverse, so rare, so soul-filling—are also so fragile that they are vulnerable to obliteration. We all at some level understand this, since we Floridians are also subject to the laws of destruction. We fight the tiny upward-chewing termites in our houses, as well as the great grand maws of hurricanes roaring toward us from across the waters. Any time a hurricane boils up on the maps over the Caribbean or the Gulf of Mexico, those among us who have read Hurston's great novel *Their Eyes Are Watching God* can see, overlaid atop the real-time hurricane as though on tracing paper, the great unnamed 1928 storm that made Lake Okeechobee overswell its bounds and drown over twenty-five hundred people.

Again and again in these great works of Florida literature, we see hurricanes; in Florida, hurricanes are the monsters under our beds. In recent years, these once-in-a-generation hurricanes have seemed to be pounding at us with greater and greater frequency; now they're no longer generational, and we are bearing up under one or two a year. What every legitimate scientist will tell us—what we know in our heart of hearts—is that climate change is occurring at a wild rate that even computerized models have a hard time forecasting. When the seas rise, the aquifer becomes salinated; when the Gulf waters warm, the coral reefs die off and leave sterility in their place; when mangroves are torn up to make way for condominiums, hurricanes have nothing to stop them from chewing up the tender littoral ecologies of both beast and man. If you have children, like I do, your worry about their futures may keep you up at night. Here's where I confess to my own incurable insomnia and dread.

This is why an intimate knowledge of climate change flavors every beautiful Florida day that I open my eyes to. It gives every run I take out on the prairie a deep poignancy. Still, I think it's possible that we can reconsider the dominant narrative we've been told, which is that nature is so fragile that it can be damaged irreparably. I think this is a dangerous story, or at the very least one that leads to the profound nonaction of despair. Because, in fact, nature wants to live. Nature is excellent at finding a way to survive. The story we should be telling is that nature is robust, and that in order to recover, our environment just needs a human hand, human ingenuity, all of the technology and money and natural resources that we are allowing eccentric billionaires to blast off into space from Cape Canaveral. As Rawlings says, "We were bred of earth before we were bred of our mothers. Once born, we can live without mother or father, or any other kin, or any friend, or any human love. We cannot live without the Earth or apart from it, and something is shriveled in a man's heart when he turns away from it and concerns himself only with the affairs of men."

It is difficult to know where to start; perhaps the first step is to sit in patience and goodwill with an interesting book that makes us see our state differently, that makes us pay attention to the small things that exist under the day-to-day bustle and worry of our lives. I am writing this now on my Gainesville porch at night after my children have gone to bed, just when the warmth and golden sunlight of the day are fading and the sliver of white moon is shyly emerging. There's a screech owl calling from the tops of the oak trees. Even in these domesticated wilds of this neighborhood, the owl's call is recognition of the mysteries out beyond the scope of the individual human's understanding, the sign of the absurd luck that despite all odds we have found ourselves right now to hear it. Maybe together we can give these moments of grace our full attention, and come to understand the astonishing fortune we share in calling Florida our home; maybe this new narrative we tell will spur us all to action.

Our Land

BUFFALO TIGER

Today, many Miccosukee people are not following their cultural beliefs about the land. They are not practicing tradition in their day-to-day lives. The young people are not taught what earth means to their lives. They need to learn and relate to the meaning and develop strong feelings like their grandfathers and their grandfathers before them. Land is more important than money. Today it seems like Indian people think other things are more important. It seems as if Miccosukees are not too concerned for the land. People need to start being concerned and turn back to their traditional practices. Our grandfathers and their grandfathers loved this earth. Because of their feelings for the land, we live here today.

Breathmaker created the earth and all living things and nature, and we are part of it. We all belong to what Breathmaker gave. Breathmaker taught us how to live on and protect the land and how to love nature. He taught us how to understand other people but to maintain our customs and culture. Breathmaker has tested us, what we are going to be, what we are going to believe. He's testing us to use written paper, to see if we can live with it. But we were not doing good. He realized that. Then he gave paper to light-skinned people, and they lived with it well. It belonged to them. It will always be that way. Then he asked us to live with nature: trees, life, and how to get along with it. We live in nature and take care of it. He told others how they must live and what they do well!

We know Florida as the "pointed land." Years and years ago people were always looking for which way to go because it was not easy for Indian people to find food and the right place to live for their people. So the wise people were sitting around all night figuring which way to go. At that time, they saw a beautiful tree standing with its limb pointing south, and that meant something. So the wise people spent time together listening to nature speaking to them, and they realized that this tree was telling us to go south. So they sent at least three fellows to check it out; they did, and they found that the "pointed land" was a beautiful place to live, so that's when they started moving down this way. So we know that's how we got here years ago. After Breathmaker had put us on earth, those things happened. We were looking for life to be better for us, so we found a place to go. But don't forget, not all of us moved down here. We lived in north Florida, around Tallahassee, and were always coming down hunting and moving around. We know this land well. Miccosukees always called it *yugnee-fuskee*. *Yugnee* is land, and *fuskee* is south—"south land"—but before that it was "pointed land." Breathmaker told us it was here for us to live on, to tend and care for.

We believed that at one time this land was underwater, but then the water drained toward the south. Big animals came down with a big man to where the land was soft. The animals could not go any farther. Different parts of this land are hard rock, coral rock, or soft rock, and in some places the rock is above ground. The east and west coasts are sandy all of the way down. In the central part, the land is soft, with rich black or gray muck. There are beautiful rivers up in the north part of the land. There also is a freshwater lake known as Lake Okeechobee.

We know plants and trees, both north and south. We know the animals and birds. We know which fish live in freshwater and which live in saltwater. We had no boundaries on this land, no fences. We were always free. All wildlife and human life could freely wander. Since Breathmaker put this land for us to live on and care for, money cannot buy land. We are not supposed to buy or sell even a cup of muck. Many of our people have fought and died for us to keep our land.

When we came down here, they found there were a lot of things people could eat. There were five different types of *yokche*, or freshwater turtles. They found things that come out of the ground that we could eat, too, like a kind of potato and coontie. There were plenty of cabbage palms. We could find seven different types of wild fruits that we could eat that grew either in the sand or out in the Glades at different times of the year. Those are the kinds of things they spotted in *yugnee-fuskee*. People wanted to come down because they realized this was the place they should live because there were lots of fruits and things to eat.

Even then, they were going back to Tallahassee, back and forth. They would live down here and hunt and then go back to Tallahassee. They had to make a move, to come down to really live here, because the troops chased them down [in the wars of the 1830s]. The elderly folks always talk about the [aboriginal] Indian people who were here before that. We called them *ouwayachee*—something that lived in the past. Our people did not expect to see them, but they were here. They went away or died. We must have killed them, or they moved away from us, so they are not here now. They established so many things like little mucky places or islands out in the Glades. They used to live in different places like that and built the ground up to live on it. We took it from them. That is the way the story is told and what we believe happened.

Soldier's Creek Trail

TERRY ANN THAXTON

She moves her hands along the trail
as if they are waves of birds
without knowing that down at the edge
where water meets sand, darkness
peeks out from behind roots.
She often wonders if she matters, but not here
where walking each day
her fingers find traces
of seed in her pockets.

She knows there is pollen on the ground.
She knows the flowers coming from the dead trunk up ahead
will soon form on her forehead.
She must look into the palm of her hand
or into this branch
which appears far away from the path,
and now she's kissing the ground and waiting
to speak, but perhaps she won't even remember
the creek, the bending copper that sings.
I have come this far, she reminds herself,
even if it doesn't seem so.

The woods offer her a log
across the creek where she could watch children,
if they were present, contradict the silence
among oaks and pines and palms. Time crosses the creek
and, just as she turns to face the ferns, she slips and becomes
a penny tossed into the water, her wrist shattered,
and she thought it couldn't hurt—
this walking all the way back,
even though she couldn't see where
she was going—a mirror of what had come
before appeared as though others
were on the trail with her—away from the light and the ferns.
Instead of this tree, it's as if
she is lifted across the creek—not the fingers
of her right hand folded into these roots
along the bank: a sling carving out her name.

PART II

REVELATIONS

Innocence Found (October 5, 1997)

BILL MAXWELL

I have a special place, a place where I read, write, and observe a group of boys fish and play on the shore of an inlet in south St. Petersburg. Sometimes only two boys show up, other times as many as seven. The youngest is probably nine, the oldest perhaps thirteen.

I spoke to three of them for the first time the other day as I was about to take a maiden voyage in my new kayak. As I pushed the sleek yellow craft into the water, the youngest boy said, "Mister, that's a nice canoe."

"It's a kayak," I said.

"A what?"

"Kayak."

But I digress.

This place is special because the boys are special. They are black. They are innocent—a quality I do not take for granted, given the powerful lure of street life in the economically depressed neighborhood where they live.

And what do these children do along this shore? They pretty much do what my friends and I did forty years ago, before television and other electronic gadgetry changed the way black boys play, when being a boy meant flying kites, shooting marbles, casting yo-yos, capturing lightning bugs, pushing car tires, playing cowboys and Indians.

These boys, like my friends and I did, invent, create, experiment, learn. They are not getting into trouble, and they apparently are thinking the thoughts that kids their ages should be thinking. Sure, they are rough-edged, and they compete—vying to see who can skip a rock on the water the farthest, who can catch the biggest sheepshead, who can stay submerged in the brackish water the longest. But their play in general lacks the serious meanness I so often see among many other black boys whom I encounter in my travels.

The mere fact that they choose to play in nature—in an area that is a gateway to the Gulf of Mexico and a window to the breathtaking Sunshine Skyway Bridge—tells me that they have a sense of beauty inside them. They, like my friends and I did, feel the pull to open spaces, where naturalness has a soothing effect, where lasting friendship based on mutual respect can be established, where openly caring for others is not laughable.

I watch them closely each time I come here. I have seen the oldest show the youngest how to make a rock jump three or four times off the surface of the water. The one who wears the Chicago Bulls jacket taught the one they call "Li'l Red" the difference between a snapper and mullet. Everyone gathers around when the tallest kid opens his slick tackle box. One afternoon, he took out something called a "wet fly" and something else called a "nymph."

I have been coming to this spot at least once a week for more than a year, beginning just after the riots that left several poor people homeless, many businesses burned, and a handful of people injured. I came the first time to get away from the newsroom and the incessant talk about the fires and the shootings. The boys also started coming here at that time. I felt that they, too, wanted to get away from the violence and the mean rhetoric around them.

The heavyset one always arrives first, sits alone on the seawall. He often brings a bag of peanuts or bread and feeds the gulls. More than a dozen of them flutter overhead, diving and screaming, as the boy tosses food into the air. From the look in his eyes, I guess that he marvels at the birds' freedom and their easy acceptance of freebies. Sometimes he talks to them, inviting the less aggressive ones to eat from his hand. He is always careful to finish this ritual before his pals arrive. This, I tell myself, is a special moment he reserves for himself.

I identify with this kid. He, like I was at his age, seems to be dreaming of things he dares not tell anyone else about. Why? Because some things are so innocent, like feeding gulls, that secrecy is the only way to protect their dignity and magic.

I distinctly feel also that the other boys in the group, who come here with fishing rods and nightcrawlers, will not tell their tough peers where they spend their time after school. After all, who would care? What could be of interest along a mangrove-lined shoreline that carries the perpetual odor of low-tide muck? How can that be cool?

Again, their innocence makes this place special for me. And on this day, dark clouds gather in the east over Tampa Bay. I want to launch the kayak, but I know the rain will fall within fifteen minutes. Plus, I see lightning in the distance over the mainland.

As I pull the kayak out of the water, the youngest boy comes over. I ask him to help me carry it back to my Blazer. He agrees.

"Grab the stern," I say.

"Where's that?"

"Back there."

"Yo, what's this thing called again?"

"A kayak. K-a-y-a-k. Kayak."

He asks if I will take him out sometime.

"You got it," I say, realizing that I will need to speak to his parents first.

The Seine

JACK E. DAVIS

In the air around us hung the commingling scents of a shallow-water estuary, the cycling living and dead of the sea.

My little sister and I stood knee-deep in Santa Rosa Sound. Scatter shots of minnows (we called all fry minnows) whizzed around our toothpick legs poking into the grassy bottom. Hunched over slightly, we each gripped a narrow bamboo staff and struggled to keep upright the attached four-foot seine net strung between as we swept it through the water and across the grass. We aimed to catch some of those minnows and anything else we could stir up.

A salesclerk showing me the seine earlier that day at the local Western Auto store said it would pull in a bounty. Colluding with a breath of cigarettes and spearmint chewing gum, his words sounded like a guarantee.

That was a long time ago, the late 1960s, in downtown Fort Walton Beach. I was eleven. "Downtown" was what we called the three blocks of storefronts across from an ancient Indian mound. A seventeen-foot-high mass of shells, fishbones, and sand, the mound sprouted twisted oaks where once stood the pine-pole and palm-thatch dwellings of an earlier civilization. The brick and mortar of the current one—which was framing, sheathing, and roofing much of the rest of Florida in a manic day-to-day onslaught—was pushing the mound and its long-vanquished people deeper into the past.

The implications of development and loss had yet to enter my consciousness. My family had recently moved to the Gulf coast from an Atlanta suburb, and my worldview had shifted from new house construction on cleared red-clay building lots to a rare spot in north Florida not yet under siege and all about water and promising adventures.

The quest for the latter had taken me to the Western Auto. The store had an impossibly vast inventory, overwhelming yet validated by its precise organization and the smell of newness. Overhead lights seemed unnecessary. Everything gleamed, most especially the row of Western Flyer bicycles with chrome fenders and Texas longhorn handlebars.

Less scintillating was the stir of a salesclerk helping a customer. I was intensely shy and didn't want anyone talking to me. The urge to leave was turning me around when I spotted the must-have accoutrement of every kid new to the water's edge. In a far corner opposite galvanized bins of nails and screws, rising in rank formation behind an aisle of windshield wipers and car soaps and waxes, were the slender tips of fishing rods. I slipped stealthily over to them. Arranged neatly on shelves were shiny baitcasting and spinning reels; chromium lures and rubbery neon ones; red-and-white plastic bobbers; tinted and clear monofilament line; sinewy-long and stubby-short wire leaders; circle hooks and calligraphic J-hooks; and lead sinkers you'd impulsively pick up to feel their compact weight. A boy with saved-up dollars in his pocket had decisions to make.

Finished with the other customer, the salesclerk approached with his waft of tobacco and mint. Considering me for a moment and somehow sensing I didn't have the wherewithal to buy a fishing rod and all that went with it, he pulled a rolled-up pole seine out of a cardboard bin. I'd never seen anything like it. He unfurled it like a flag and fingered the sinkers that ran along the lower course. Leaning over, he demonstrated how to grip the bamboo staffs affixed to each end, as with a baseball bat but with hands wide apart. This was a man practiced at moving inventory. "A couple a runs through the grass, and you and a buddy'll get yourselves a bucket a swimmers and the like." He nodded toward the mound across the street. "This here's the same kind a net they used. The Indians that lived 'round here." He fixed his eyes on his young customer and said nothing more, waiting for him to bite and affirm the self-satisfaction already curled into his smile.

I bit.

Hours later, I coaxed and cajoled my sister into the seagrass to put the salesclerk's promise to test. I was in cut-off jeans, light-blue ones—I wore no others—and a white T-shirt that I couldn't wear to school because the bold-red Budweiser logo on the front might corrupt my sixth-grade classmates (in my one appearance at school in the shirt, Mrs. Edwins, the principal, a blocky force of sternness, made me turn it inside out). I had on old tennis shoes, PF Flyers knockoffs, with the front of the canvas tops cut off to let in cool air when on land and let out water when on the flats. Bare feet were an ambulatory hazard. Painful sandspurs hid in patchy ground, and razor-edged oysters in the water. You were always walking in the water, living where I did on the western reach of the Florida panhandle.

Until I heard the sales pitch at the Western Auto, it had not occurred to me that people had been fishing the same way in these waters for millennia. Compared with the size and strength of the nets that native mound builders fashioned from marsh grasses, mine barely qualified as featherweight. It was a "Made in Japan" mass-produced import, cheaply manufactured with thin cotton line and prone to twist up in a knot. The man promised a bounty, nevertheless. If a bounty is dozens of baby shrimp, half as many fry, and a small blue crab, then we pulled in a bounty. It was to me. I gave no thought to its source, the estuary we were wading through.

We lived footsteps away from those seine-netted shallows. Our house, built from durable Alabama and Florida pine, stood something like a sovereign over them. It had two stories, each spanned by a screened porch open to fresh sea air and a panorama of Santa Rosa Sound. Two hundred yards wide and drawing east and west, the sound was like a straight and lazy river between the mainland and a narrow barrier island. The Gulf washed into Choctawhatchee Bay at the east end and Pensacola Bay at the west. The forty miles between were mostly empty back then. Lone tugboats periodically pushed rust-fouled cargo barges along their course. They were silent movers outside the steady drone of their engines, which on a south wind would send a draught of diesel smell our way. A half mile to our west, the tugs ran behind a small spoil island built from sand dredged from the bottom of the sound to deepen the barge channel. When I got my first boat, a red-fiberglass twelve-foot square-back canoe with a gray-and-white six-horsepower Johnson outboard, I was a frequent visitor of that island, taking with me my dog Lulu, a liver-and-white springer spaniel.

The water around the spoil was clear and alive. Schools of fish and casts of hermit crabs were an urban bustle in its sandy shallows. A stingray would occasionally skate in and part the multitudes. Drawn by them, air squadrons of brown pelicans flew silently at low altitudes on search-and-feed missions. Brush and dune grass grew across the spine of spoil sand, and marsh grass around portions of it, but no seagrass beds to speak of in its waters. The seine stayed in the boat.

The sound and its estuarine habitat turned out to be this other world beyond my sandspur yard, as were woods to baby-boomer kids living in green-lawn neighborhoods. But I didn't know enough to think of the island's marsh grass as a living place with much of the same surprises the seine revealed in other places.

One of those was Pirates Cove, across the barge channel from the island. Getting there was a risky affair if a tug was driving through, yet exciting if you turned the boat full speed into the tug's heaving wake and put air between hull and water. The cove was hidden at the end of a natural channel that twisted like a secret through a palisade of reedy marsh grass. From the hushed enclosed interior, where only a lone jumping mullet broke the silence, Santa Rosa Sound and the tug barges were nowhere in sight. I never boated into the cove without a friend. There was too much mystery in it, too many wild imaginings inspired by it, including the reason for its name. Less disquieting, it was also an altar of nature, with infinite opportunities to run the seine and bring in bait shrimp to fish with.

One summer afternoon, hot under the sun, noses and shoulders beaming red, a friend named Bobby and I ventured into the cove. Toward the far side from the entrance, we spotted a prehistoric monster loitering in the water. We jumped out of the boat with the seine. Bobby sloshed around to one side of the monster and I the other. It didn't stir. We swept it into the net, which the creature's length nearly filled. Back in the boat, it remained docile as we raced out of the cove as fast as the Johnson's six horses would move us, crossed the barge channel—no tugs in sight—and over to the house of a neighbor, a retired air force colonel. A very important person to us, he'd be able to identify our catch with its coarse, brutal-looking skin and gnarly snout. He said we had netted an alligator gar, and, no, we could not eat it. It appeared to be dead by this time anyway. We took it off in the boat and dropped it lifeless into the sound a hundred yards out from the front of my house.

All the homeowners referred to the waterside as the front. Claiming the view straight across the sound from ours was Santa Rosa Island (we knew it as Okaloosa Island), longer than the sound and about as wide, mostly undeveloped—because the military owned it—dead quiet, pure white, all sand and stillness, dunes out of *Arabian Nights*, bald under bristles of amber-and-green sea oats. It was a picture.

The vast Gulf was on the south side of the island. The local chamber of commerce claimed that the panhandle had the best ocean beaches in the world. It was a cliché but not a stretch. They were broad and uncluttered, singularly white and flawless, the sand sun-warmed and afternoon-nap soft. The tourism people called the color of the water emerald, and you wondered whether the Caribbean was as scintillating. Out on the beach, we'd let the sheets of coming-in water chase us across the tidal sand. We in turn chased sand crabs into their burrows. Once old enough, we surfed spiraling waves, and used the slope of the dunes to invent sand skiing.

On hot summer nights, I slept on a field-hospital cot on the upstairs porch of our big sovereign house. The cot's yellowing canvas, stretched military-taut across an ash-wood frame, hurt my bony shoulders when I lay on my side. But I slept. I slept in the Gulf's cool breeze that carried over the island and dunes, across the sound and past our creosoted dock, snare-drumming the fronds on our one sabal palm, shushing through the salt-corroded screen. I slept to the distant white noise of the breakers, deeply in dreams, until birdsong woke me in the morning.

On the other side, the north side, of our house was the coastal highway, U.S. 98, nicknamed the Miracle Strip, another chamber of commerce invention. In the yard around our drive, the outstretched limbs of old live oaks shouldered swags of Spanish moss that muted the road noise. There was no baby-boomer neighborhood, no cul-de-sac streets with a circus of kids on bicycles and skates. No pick-up football or baseball games on front lawns.

My sister was pretty much the landlubber and into her own activities. I was alone most of the time, except for Lulu, but never bored. Nor was she. She was the consummate fisher, boat rider, and dock snoozer. Santa Rosa Sound was the cul-de-sac of my youth. Docks were the sidewalks, waterways the streets, the little motorboat my bicycle, and a rod and reel my bat and ball.

It wasn't until much later that I realized how privileged I had been to live where I did. I'm not referring to waterfront luxury. My family was modestly middle class, and waterfront property was affordable to many more then. I'm talking about the estuary at my doorstep, open and uncrowded by people and buildings, all but to myself, a surplus of attractions for an adolescent's fidgeti-ness. We moved from New England to Birmingham to Atlanta before ending up on this water. It was the first place where I valued relationships with people less than with non-people: the gamboling blue crabs and lumbering hermit crabs, the endlessly leaping mullet, the skydiving pelicans (plunging for the mullet), the pinwheeling bottlenose dolphins (chasing the mullet), the oper-atic wind outside that sang arias through our old but resilient house during Hurricane Camille, the toadfish that lived like a pet next to a dock piling, the nibbling when I bathed off the end of the dock with a bar of soap my mother gave me.

We didn't know it at the time, but clean waters were a rare commodity in those days. At the western reach of the sound, Pensacola was beset by the murkiness of the age. Municipalities near and far—upriver in other states—spilled and pumped nitrogen-rich raw sewage and industrial effluent into rivers and streams that spilled to bays and bayous and exploded them with algae blooms that killed fish and crabs and sent away the feeding birds and dolphins. We were lucky; the ogre of population growth and the worst of humanity's ceaseless endeavors had mostly spared us, left us with a wealth unrecorded on corporate spreadsheets and with a quality of life vacated by the hyper-materialism consuming most of America.

Before my sister and I swept the seine through the shallows that first time, I had never liked seagrass. It was slimy, alien, and haunted by unseen biting and pinching things. But this was the grass's point, its reason for being, larger than our quest, larger than our lifetimes, larger than the centuries between us and the aboriginal mound builders, larger than our human kind. And more important.

How was I to know?

We took nature's providence for granted. Neither my teachers, nor my parents, spoke of estuaries or ecosystems. Biodiversity, microbial communities, carbon exchange, dinoflagellates, and hypoxia weren't topics of conversation. Macroalgae, yes, but only in the name of seaweed. I could not answer two basic questions: what is an estuary and why are they important to life on earth, including human life?

I can now. Despite its flimsiness, the seine delivered the answers with each run through the grass. It showed me something I might never have seen, not in my impressionable years, not in years that followed. It delivered an awareness and retention that shapes the way I came to view the world, one world, not separate human and nonhuman worlds, one world.

My First Audubon Trip Hasn't Ended Yet . . .

CHARLES LEE

Shortly after my sixteenth birthday, my mother drove me to Key West where I joined a group from the Florida Audubon Society embarking to the Dry Tortugas, a group of islands seventy miles to the west. The group would spend two weeks banding and counting Sooty and Noddy Terns nesting on Bush Key, an island a few hundred yards to the east of Garden Key, where the massive brick polygon, Fort Jefferson, towers over adjacent waters. We were to stay in the fort, long since turned over to the National Park Service by the military. The fort, built over several decades during the nineteenth century, is the largest brick structure in the Western Hemisphere. It served as a prison for notable characters that the U.S. government wanted to isolate from the mainland. In 1865, Dr. Samuel Mudd and several other Lincoln assassination conspirators were imprisoned there.

From about the age of fourteen I had been active in conservation issues in South Florida. My interest was spurred by a love for fishing in Biscayne Bay. By the time I was thirteen I had an old aluminum johnboat with a five-horsepower outboard motor and explored the twisted mangrove streams that were tributaries to the northern part of the bay. One by one I found my isolated fishing holes, which were loaded with mangrove snapper, snook, and tarpon, filled in or dredged out by developers creating new dry land for housing projects. I developed a gnawing sense that this could not go on forever or there would be nothing left. I started writing letters to the editor of the *Miami News*, then the evening newspaper in Miami. My letters described the destruction and called for action to save the bay. I was surprised but pleased when most were published.

One day my mother got a telephone call from one of the leaders of the Mangrove Chapter of the Izaak Walton League, a group fighting against dredging and filling in Biscayne Bay. They talked for a while and then she put me on the phone. The caller was surprised that I was just a kid, but he asked if I could come to one of the group's meetings. My mother drove me there. At the meeting and many others to follow, I became acquainted with the people leading the nascent environmental movement in South Florida, among them Jim Redford, Polly Redford, Lloyd Miller, and Alice Wainwright. Alice invited me to a meeting of the Tropical Audubon Society. It was at that Audubon meeting that I learned about the bird-banding trip to the Dry Tortugas. I sheepishly asked if I could go along. I was surprised when they said yes.

So, the old rusty and gray former U.S. Navy buoy tender owned by the National Park Service plodded west toward the Dry Tortugas. At its top speed of six knots, it would take about ten hours to get there. I must admit that my enthusiasm for joining a bird banding trip was fired up by an ulterior motive. The Dry Tortugas was a legendary sport fishing paradise. I had only heard of the Tortugas by reading articles in magazines like *Outdoor Life* and *Field and Stream* and knew it was a place were only a few rich and famous fishing pros could afford to go. Now I was going there, and I had my fishing rod with me.

There were two places to fish on Garden Key: one was the pier where incoming boats docked, in a magnificent deep-blue channel coming straight out of the Gulf Stream. The other was the "coaling docks," which consisted of twisted and rusted remains of a steel pier that once refueled warships. The battleship USS *Maine* left those docks in February 1898 for its ill-fated last voyage to Cuba. In the channel I hooked into huge snapper and grouper. At the coaling docks were massive tarpon and amberjack. I fished every day from about eleven in the morning until about three in the afternoon. For a sixteen-year-old, Garden Key was a fishing paradise.

We banded terns in the early morning hours before the heat put stress on netted birds. We also banded in the late afternoon when the sun was low. Noted ornithologists Dr. William B. Robertson and Dr. John Ogden were in charge of the operation. There were about ten of us recruited from Audubon who helped. Banding adult birds was accomplished by stretching thin mist nets between metal conduit pipes driven into the sand. Banding chicks required catching them by hand. The chick banding part was tough work, with a lot of crawling around in brush. The younger folks were assigned to that task. The mist net capture of adult birds was much more interesting. One afternoon I heard Robertson talking loudly over by the nets. That was unusual because he was a really quiet and reserved fellow. I took a break and crawled out from under the brush to see what was going on. They had captured a Sooty Tern with an old U.S. Fish and Wildlife Service band on its leg. The bird was over thirty years old, and had been banded in the 1930s.

Gradually, I moved up the food chain in the banding crew from chasing chicks under bushes to helping a marine biologist from the University of Miami collect bird puke from terns captured in the net. Most birds were caught when coming in from the open ocean after filling their gullets with small fish found in the yellow sargassum weed lines of the Gulf Stream. When the birds hit the nets and became entangled, many barfed up their catch. Depending on how long the small fish were in the gullet of the tern, some specimens left hanging in the nets or dropping to the ground beneath the birds could be quite fresh, almost alive. My job was to gather the whole undigested specimens and place them in jars of formaldehyde. These fish were not ordinary minnows. The small fish living close to the surface in weed lines include tiny juvenile versions of the world's greatest gamefish. Among the tiny fish cradled in my hand on the way to the smelly formaldehyde jar were small-scale copies of bluefin tuna, king mackerel, wahoo, sailfish, marlin, and dolphin. As a boy who came to the Tortugas motivated by fishing, my admiration for birds, and understanding of their role in the ecosystem, was crystalized on the sands of Bush Key while looking at these miraculous specimens.

It was in the makeshift kitchen and dining room at Fort Jefferson that I became fascinated with the Audubon Society and the older members I was privileged to mingle with. While most of the older members of the crew parked their cots in the plywood-walled sleeping quarters on the first floor facing the fort's ten-acre parade ground, I made camp on the second floor, where a seemingly endless series of brick arches opened to views over the water. Crescent-shaped iron tracks on the rough stone floor in these quarters once allowed wheeled cannons to swing back and forth. I tied my cot to one of the tracks to keep the breeze from blowing it away.

One morning, Robertson gathered us at breakfast with a worried look. The Tortugas were in the path of approaching Hurricane Alma. No evacuation was possible; the old park service buoy tender could never outrun the storm. We would have to stay and ride it out. The eye of the hurricane, preceded by 130-mile-per-hour winds, passed directly over Fort Jefferson on June 8, 1966. For about a day and a half we were holed up in a brick chamber on the lower level. A sign pointed toward Dr. Mudd's cell. Over one of the archways were etched the words "Whoso entereth here leaveth all hope behind."

I frequently ventured outside for a few minutes at a time, even during the height of the storm, and found protected vantage points from which I could view the action in its full glory. When the eye passed over, everyone went outside to look for birds, lured by the numerous legends of extraordinary bird finds associated with the passing of a hurricane. Soon shrieks and yells could be heard across the parade ground as the dark eyewall of Alma approached. The approaching clouds were accompanied by a rumbling "freight train" sound. The howls were not, however, related to the approaching maelstrom. Rather, all eyes were fixed on the white-tailed tropicbird soaring above the fort, and black swifts and gray-rumped swifts darting above the open parade ground: rare sightings ranked as once-in-a-lifetime events for most birders. The whole crew stayed out far too long and had to lean hard into the wind and endure a pounding by stinging rain while struggling back toward the calm of the brick fortress.

One of the people I shared Hurricane Alma with was C. Russell Mason. In a number of long and winding conversations, Mason instilled in me the desire to spend my life in conservation work.

The story that most intrigued me was how he and some Audubon friends helped save the Florida population of bald eagles.

Mason came back to Florida in 1957 to take the job as executive director of Florida Audubon. At that time, devastating impacts to ecosystems and the cascade of multiple species toward extinction were just beginning to be recognized. Mason was not exactly a newcomer to Audubon. He had once before presided at Florida Audubon as its volunteer president from 1936 to 1940 at a time when the organization had no staff. Mason was stationed in Sanford, Florida, as manager of the Florida office of the Stokes Seed Company. His love of birds was intertwined with his educational background in agriculture. He received his undergraduate degree in horticulture from Pennsylvania State University, and his masters in horticulture from Purdue University. Through his employment, Mason gained an appreciation for Florida farmers and landowners and the challenges they faced. In 1940, he went to Massachusetts to accept a job as executive director of the Massachusetts Audubon Society, where he served for seventeen years. But the lure of Florida always tugged at him, so when recruited for the job in 1957 by Florida Audubon stalwarts Lisa Von Borowsky and John Storer, he quickly packed his bags.

Mason told me how he and his Audubon members began an effort to conduct one of the first exhaustive surveys to identify active bald eagle nests in Florida. He described one Audubon volunteer, George Heinzman, who brought to Audubon a particularly valuable set of skills—the ability to mingle with and gain the confidence and respect of cattle ranchers. Mason said he had been unable to gain access to cattle ranches to do the eagle survey until Heintzman appeared. Heinzman had been a wildcat trucker, lumberman, furniture sales-man, and banker. He had wandered extensively throughout the western United States and had an intense interest in the history of that region and the early days of the cattle industry there. Heinzman authored a historical novel, *Powder River Cowman*, published by Macmillan in 1962. The novel chronicles events from the 1870s through the 1890s in the Powder River Basin of Montana and northeast Wyoming. Heinzman knew cowmen, could speak in their terms, and even looked a bit like a cowpoke character actor from central casting, rather than a "do-gooder" from the Audubon Society.

Heintzman gained the cooperation of the ranchers and with that came ac-cess to the ranches so the survey could be completed. Ultimately, the survey revealed that about 250 bald eagle nests remained active in Florida, nearly half the entire U.S. population. Most of the nests were located in just three Florida counties: Osceola, Polk, and Okeechobee.

Mason and Heinzman moved forward to formalize cooperation between ranchers and Audubon to protect this highly important eagle nest stronghold. They launched the creation of the "Kissimmee Cooperative Bald Eagle Sanc-tuary," a voluntary program in which ranchers would sign a letter agreeing to protect eagles and nests on their property and post their property with distinc-tive metal yellow signs declaring it to be a bald eagle sanctuary in coopera-tion with Audubon. Audubon provided the ranchers with educational material about eagles and suggestions for managing areas in proximity to eagle nest trees.

By October 1962, fifty-nine of the largest cattle ranch owners, whose proper-ties encompassed more than 600,000 acres, had signed up for the program and posted the signs. The Florida Audubon Society published an article beginning on the front cover of its *Florida Naturalist* magazine, which was later reprinted in whole or part in newspapers across the country, including the *New York Times*. The article listed the names of the ranch families that had signed up to declare their lands eagle sanctuaries, and included a map showing the general location of the lands protected by agreement between the City of Kissimmee and Lake Okeechobee. I was truly inspired by the story.

In 1972, I was privileged to be offered a job at Florida Audubon by Hal Scott, the executive director who followed Mason in that position. One of my first assignments was to fight the Marco Island development of the Mackle Brothers' Deltona Corporation that threatened to fill in thousands of acres of mangrove wetlands. The project had already received all its state permits. The U.S. Army Corps of Engineers' approval was the last permit the company needed. Audubon friend and confidant Nathaniel Reed, who then served as U.S. Assistant Secretary of the Department of Interior, had warned me that there wasn't much chance of the Corps denying the permit because Mackle associate Bebe Rebozo was President Richard Nixon's close friend. Reed told me I should hope for a miracle, because I needed one.

Not long after that conversation, my telephone rang. The miracle had begun to happen. On the line was a man named Jack Eckerd. The name sounded familiar, but I could not place it. Then I remembered: Eckerd owned the biggest chain of drug stores in Florida. He had run for Florida governor in 1970 but had lost the Republican primary. One of the people behind his defeat was Deltona's Frank Mackle. Eckerd wanted to know how he could help us stop the Marco Island dredge-and-fill permits. Ultimately, he agreed to fund a publicity campaign against the permit, including full-page ads in all major Florida newspapers. The campaign helped sway decision makers, and two years later the Deltona permit was denied.

My career continues with Audubon and is always rewarding. Whether the next day brings an important achievement or setback, I know it will bring adventure, and the chance to do something, big or small, to help the birds, the fish, the wetlands, and wild places. The phone calls and opportunities continue to happen, and occasionally some miracles occur.

By the way, in case you were wondering, although I was only sixteen, my mother wasn't too worried about me during Hurricane Alma. Alice Wainwright had called the National Park Service and relayed the news that I would be safe from the storm near Dr. Mudd's cell inside the largest brick structure in the Western Hemisphere.

Florida Boy

DAVID MCCALLY

*Under heaven all can see beauty as beauty only because
there is ugliness.
All can know good as good only because there is evil.*

When men lack a sense of awe, there will be disaster.

–Lao Tsu

Aside from unsurveyed tracts in the Everglades, Florida has only scattered patches of truly wild land. The state's forests have all been logged, and what we see today can be no better than second growth. Indeed, all too often beautification strips line our highways, giving the illusion of a forest, while concealing the silviculture that supplies the planted pines demanded mostly by paper mills. These tree farms no more equal forests than do cornfields equal meadows. In the same vein, multiuse mandates mean that even state and national forests offer visitors managed environments while conservation lands, too, have been altered by human hands, although they do offer the hope of wild lands in the future.

At any rate, parks and conserved lands have little to offer urban children, especially if their families cannot afford vacations. During my own childhood, my mother (who graduated from high school the same year I did) struggled alone to provide decent lives for her children. I do recall one long weekend camping at Munson Recreational Area with a borrowed tent and Coleman stove and lantern, but for the most part I had to rely on my imagination and the local landscape to become acquainted with the natural world. I grew up in Pensacola, a city that followed the typical Florida pattern of low-density development coupled with quickly abandoned aging properties. Luckily for me, the vicinity of the adjacent neighborhoods of East Hill, which adjoins Bayou Texar on the west, and East Pensacola Heights, a peninsula with the bayou on its western side and Pensacola Bay to the east, offered a wide array of neglected or abandoned land, and my free-range childhood gave me the opportunity to explore.

Bayou Texar, fed by Carpenters Creek, winds its way through eastern Pensacola for a couple of miles until it empties into Pensacola Bay at the 17th Avenue trestle. Seen from the bridge that connects East Hill with East Pensacola Heights, the bayou looks like a small bay whose calm waters hosted water-skiing tournaments when I was an adolescent, but less than a mile away, to the southwest, it narrows to a channel no more than twenty-five yards wide where treacherous currents have caused a surprising number of drownings. The shoreline between the bridge and the bayou's mouth provided my friends and me with a scene for many adventures, as did the spoil island alongside the boat channel to the bay. This island could be reached from the east side of the bayou by wading during low tide, and we loved to explore its thick stand of reeds and sedges.

While poking around one memorable afternoon we heard the low rumble, not quite a growl, that a gator might make when alarmed. We looked at each other, hesitated, and then did our best imitation of the Keystone Kops scrambling to get back to shore, where we stood chattering with excitement, swearing we would never go out *there* again. Of course, we did, but only after about ten minutes of rock throwing, our universal response to danger—and, I believe, a human signature that warns other species to clear out, as when a Maasai youth disperses lions menacing his village's herd with a rock from a sling. The gator did, indeed, depart but left behind not only its body's impression in the soft muck—it must have been at least ten feet long—but also a sense of wonder still vivid in my mind as I write these words.

The bayou also allowed us to amuse ourselves by honing our dormant gatherer-hunter skills. We went crabbing in the daytime, using a chicken back attached to a piece of clothesline. One of us would throw out the line, wait for a nibble, then slowly draw the crab close enough for a buddy manning the scoop net to catch it. It's surprising how nimbly crabs avoided that net. When we did manage to catch a dozen or so, John Dahlin's mother would make the best deviled crabs I have ever had, provided that we picked the meat for her. During the summertime twilight, the bayou's shoreline teemed with lightning bugs, and we caught all we could in a jar, until the streetlights blinked on and we all knew to go home. At night, we could occasionally persuade our parents that we could be trusted with sharp objects in the dark, and we would go gigging flounder in the bayou's shallows, locating them with a flashlight beam while they slept on the bottom.

While we did catch some fish, on many nights we lost interest in the tedium of the hunt and instead fooled around with the frog gig, throwing it around like madmen, with only a moderate degree of success at actually managing to spear anything, and giving lie to all the promises we had made about safety. In the mornings we often saw bird tracks on the bayou's small beaches, along with those of an occasional snake. On an afternoon's lark, Buddy Skipper pinned a minnow to the bottom with his gig's tines, picked up the fish, then, in front of god and everybody, swallowed the poor thing. He told me later that he thought he might puke, but he had certainly distinguished himself among his fellows that day.

Following the shoreline south led to the mouth of the bayou, which offered a choice: turn west and go into the rail yard, or go east and follow the tracks to the bluffs. The east led to the distinguishing feature of Pensacola Bay–eroded clay bluffs rising as high as sixty feet before falling abruptly to a narrow strip of land that provides right-of-way for railroad tracks, buttressed by a seawall and granite boulders. In contrast, turning west led to a short trestle crossing the bayou, and then into a rail yard. There must have been at least twenty sidings in those days, with rolling stock parked on many of them. The cars in the front ranks drew little interest, simply modern freight cars waiting for use, but behind them lay a whole world of antique bunkhouse cars, cook shack cars, and cabooses, as well as freight cars damaged by derailment. We marveled at the deformities of the mangled cars but found the antique cars irresistible. We explored inside, found hobo beds, and once encountered a raccoon, a surprisingly formidable adversary at close range.

But even here, in this neglected industrial area, we encountered the natural world. Numerous ant lions made their homes, perfectly shaped cones, in the sandy area near the railroad embankment. We learned to use a pine needle to disturb the cone's sand just enough to fool the ant lion into coming from the bottom of the cone, its miniature crab claws snapping in hopes of catching an ant for its dinner. Horned toads, too, patrolled these sandy areas, because they ate ants themselves. In the ditches, a bit further away from the tracks, stood pitcher plants of a species, "Infrequent to rare in a few bogs and low open areas of west Florida and adjacent areas of other states," according to *Florida Wild Flowers and Roadside Plants*, and another rare one found only "in a few localities in two or three western most counties" in Florida as well as in scattered patches from Mississippi to the Carolinas, according to the same source. Pitcher plants hold water, and a number of B movies prepared me to like best the ones with an insect floating inside. Golden Orb spiders found the abandoned cars a congenial site for their homes, and they too could be tricked into believing a meal could be had by tossing the end of a pine needle into their webs. Their quickness always startled those of us who had not seen them move before.

My buddies and I had a great time among the rolling stock, but only a few of them would make the long walk to the bluffs, so I often went with my sister. Brenda and I had such a close bond as children that we would not tell on each other's misdemeanors, neither to our mother nor to any other authority, if it came to that, prompting my mother to declare us "thicker than thieves." Brenda was lithe, lean, and spirited. She would endure the walk just to have the chance to show me she could do anything I could, and sometimes do it better. She could best me at tree climbing, for instance, because she was smaller and lighter, which allowed her to go higher on more slender limbs. I thought she knew no fear, until decades later she acknowledged that the whole time I hollered for her to come down she was trembling. Even in adulthood she couldn't, or wouldn't, explain what prompted her to take the risks. I suppose my exasperated mother knew the truth when she acknowledged after one of our misadventures that "what's born in the bone can't be beaten out of the flesh."

For a child, being down in among the bluffs seemed a magical place, a series of secluded valleys separated by steep hog backs of clay, which ranged in color from a sandy brown to deep red. Along this area of the bay front, only Gull Point offered enough flat land for early settlement, and people still lived there, some in period houses. There was also a creosote works, abandoned years ago, and a defunct train station, with a walk-in safe, its huge door swung open, which seemed both mysterious and ominous to our young eyes. The brick "old chimney," as it is known locally, which stands as the point's best-known landmark, can be seen from old U.S. 90 (designated "Scenic Highway"); it represented the only survivor of an otherwise vanished brickworks. Although unknown to me at the time, these works left their marks on the bluffs where workers quarried clay by removing the hog backs and digging back as near to the highway right-of-way as they dared, leaving behind what western movies had taught us to view as box canyons, with a sheer side abutting the highway right-of-way. The excavators left narrow terraces in these manmade cliffs in order to avoid landslides, which we delighted in using to cross from one side of the canyon to the other. This usually entailed stepping from one terrace to another, since few of the paths stretched all the way across. My fearless sister would go anywhere I dared, even though these crossings favored long legs and arms. Being so close to the cliff face during our crossings, we could not help but notice the thin strata of seeping clay, some no more than a quarter-inch thick, that ranged in color from white to pink to mauve, while others were black and even green, all stacked distinctly atop one another amidst the predominate red clay.

In a time before video games, we had to make our own fun, and while at the bluffs our imaginations got as much exercise as our legs. When we crossed on cliff terraces, we were in the Himalayas; when we found hillside groves of pines where needles had collected into deep beds, we were bandits on the lam, or, just one time, Castro's guerrillas resting in the mountains. The secluded train station took us to the Old West, while the nearby turpentine works, with its stave-lined pits filled with murky water and its charred freestanding cement passageways, seemed so alien that we felt we must be on another planet. In favorite places we built forts, only to emerge at the sound on a train's horn to throw rocks at an imagined enemy. Once I saw an alligator that had strayed into the bay from some river (the Escambia, Blackwater, and Yellow rivers empty into the bay) only to end up on the granite rocks below the sea wall, thrashing around violently in either disappointment or fury at finding itself on such a hostile shore, prompting us to think of ourselves as big-game hunters in a desperate struggle. We also often saw dolphins following shrimp boats that could still fish the bay, the wily mammals feeding on the marine life that evaded their nets, or we might catch sight of one of the white squirrels that abound in the vicinity of East Pensacola Heights. As we explored the bluffs, the real world intertwined with our imaginations to create a low-tech virtual reality where we made all sorts of conquests and discoveries.

The world seemed newer then, but surely young eyes create a newer, younger world. I believe that this aspect of human perception makes environmental advocacy all the more difficult. Certainly, in Florida, rapid population growth means people have different starting dates for their environmental reality. Additionally, many of the state's citizens have never seen this land through the eyes of a child, which leads them to a too-ready acceptance of today's suburban or even exurban sprawl as simply part of the landscape. As a child I certainly accepted things as they existed as the way things should be; it was only as an adult that I understood the effect of the brick works on the bluffs. But as an adult, my childhood experiences in the natural world, no matter how much altered, gives me a depth of perspective so often lacking among Floridians. For instance, green anoles, abundant when I was a child, have become a rarity, replaced by brown ones. Horned toads have disappeared, perhaps victims to the war on fire ants, and it would be unsurprising to find invasive coyotes living in the bluffs. I also know that low-density development created the neglected spaces where I explored the natural world. A trap-door spider does not care if it builds its lair in an old-growth forest, a rural home site, or an abandoned brown field, so long as the habitat provides the insects it needs to feed itself and its young. Nature neither has a final destination, nor does it stand still, but environmental change caused by the increasing power of human agency can be ignored only at our peril, especially in Florida.

The River That Raised Me

GABBIE BUENDIA

Summer (2019)

Some months had passed since I had seen the river. I knew that I was due for a visit, but the heat and stick of August weighed me down to my bed and deterred me from wandering outside any time past 10 AM. I was determined, however, to fight my summer slump and make a trip to bid the river "goodbye"—at least for now.

Trudging through the traffic by the University of Central Florida and sliding through scattered suburban developments, I inched my way into Oviedo to reach the Econ River Wilderness Area. A trail through this 240-acre preserve leads visitors through pine flatwoods and oak hammocks straight to the Econlockhatchee River.

A major tributary of the St. Johns River, the Econlockhatchee—or the Econ, as it is locally and lovingly known—flows for fifty-five miles. It weaves through three counties, including my home of Seminole County. The ecological value of the river has earned it Outstanding Florida Water status from the state and has ensured its protection through a series of preserves, national forests, scenic trails, and other wild areas. It is in these varied spaces that I have come to know the Econ and have learned to find awe and comfort in a landscape that once brought me fear and anxiety.

Fall (2014)

I was introduced to the Econ during what I consider to be my first-ever hike, at the age of seventeen. When my dear friend Amy called to invite me on a hike,

I was actually a bit confused. To me, "hiking" brought images of mountains, heavy boots, and long treacherous days that climaxed with rugged voyagers nodding at a scenic view, walking stick in hand. Well . . . I knew there were no mountains in Florida. And the only closed-toed shoes I had were an old pair of Nikes. And I did not at all find myself "rugged" enough to make it to that final scene. With those ideas in mind, I was left scared and nervous, fully not knowing what to expect.

My perceptions of how to enjoy natural spaces and what kind of people enjoyed them were greatly misinformed. They were influenced by limited access to positive environmental experiences growing up and a lack of representation of people of color in the outdoor spaces and activities that I did have the chance to participate in. Even though I was interested in the natural world and did appreciate some of the time I spent outdoors, I often found myself unprepared and out of place in such situations. Because of this, I struggled to understand the value of and form a deep connection with natural spaces until I got older.

Despite this, the excitement of catching up with an old friend won me over, and I got geared up to go. When I joined Amy in the passenger seat of her family's SUV, a quick transition from strip malls to sod farms marked our approach to the Little Big Econ State Forest. Finally pulling up to the trailhead, I became aware of my lack of preparedness. As I stepped out anxiously donning my cheerleading practice gear, Amy kindly extended to me her extra sunscreen, bug spray, and granola. The generosity and gentleness with which she introduced me to the space eased my nerves as we began our trek.

This particular path to the Econ is part of the Florida National Scenic Trail and exemplifies the unique beauties of Central Florida. Its high and dry sand pathways are bordered by saw palmettos and a variety of native pines, exemplifying the highlands that have attracted cattle ranching to the region both historically and in current times. The sand path eventually darkens under the cover of an oak hammock before transforming into the steep banks of the river. These high banks shield the river from view and beckon travelers to the trail's edge for a peek down into creeping amber waters. The pace and hue of the river is attributed to the relatively level topography of Florida, which causes slow flows and allows for the leaching of plant nutrients and their colored tannins into the water. Accentuated by the midday sunlight, the deep tones of the river tie together the beige, green, and brown palette of the surrounding landscape.

As Amy and I treaded down the path, my initial reactions and emotions were mixed. I was, to some degree, underwhelmed by the discovery that hiking wasn't necessarily some sort of life-altering mental and physical test in the wild. Turns out that hiking could be a moderate stroll accompanied by quality time with a friend and all of the other beings of the outdoors. Not as glorious, but still extremely satisfying. At the same time, I still carried fear with me. Keeping a few steps behind Amy, I hesitated to follow when she climbed trees to see a better view or when she headed toward more challenging paths. At one point, a snake appeared on the path and brought me so much anxiety that we could not continue until Amy put me on her back and jumped over it for the both of us. Despite all of this, I did find that I was enjoying myself. The delight of jumping over puddles on the path, balancing on fallen tree trunks, and spotting tiny toads and insects on the forest floor elicited a strange feeling of nostalgia for childhood memories that I had not actually experienced. Before I could understand what was happening, each new frightened, anxious, and delighted step was reframing my perceptions and understanding of "hiking," natural spaces, and where I fit into it all.

Winter (2018)

Inspired by that first hike, I spent my college years slowly and timidly learning more about Florida's natural spaces. The more experience I got in the outdoors and in the classroom, the more I came to understand the processes and daily happenings of my natural environment. I also met other young people of color who had held similar mixed sentiments for the outdoors growing up. Together, we learned about how our country's history of exclusion and racism impacted our experiences with natural spaces. Then, we reimagined what being a "naturalist" or "environmentalist" meant and crafted ways to enjoy the outdoors on our own terms. By my senior year, this greater understanding and new community brought me to a comfort level that encouraged continued exploration. Quickly accessible to the suburbs where I worked and played, the river easily became a frequent pause in the hectic schedule and expectations of senior year.

As I set my intentions on exploration, I sought out new locations and features of the Econ River to appreciate, and soon found my favorite spot. Venturing toward what seemed to be a dead-end path at the Econ River Wilderness Area carried me into the core of the river's floodplain forest. The drought of winter left the river low and the floodplain dry, exposing the roots and sand that gave the river shape. A network of cypress knees creeped and poked out of the sand, inviting me to step into the ghost of the river. This field of bony roots opened up to a usually inaccessible sliver of sand along the river that I could not resist following. I climbed, and slid, and plodded along the edge of the tannic flow, through sand and mud and water to a true dead end. Here, a feeling of childlike nostalgia swept over me once again, as I took pause in the midst of the deep and beautiful secrets of the river.

· · ·

Exploring didn't always go so smoothly or peacefully, though. Another day during my finals that year, I woke up with some extra time before class and decided to take a morning tour of the Econlockhatchee Sandhills Conservation Area. I arrived just as the morning dew was beginning to sparkle and evaporate off of the saw palmetto and gopher apple shrubs. The chill of winter sharpened the smell of dry pine needles and gave the grass underfoot an icy crunch. I laughed with a visibly frosty exhale, as I imagined the clumps of greenish-gray deer moss on the forest floor as bubbles immersing the forest in a bubble bath.

With no sun or mosquitoes to fend off, I took my time drifting through unfamiliar paths and smiling at new imaginations of the landscape. Eventually, the scenes became a little too unfamiliar, and I realized I was lost. Retracing my steps only brought me to more unknown areas, and my phone's GPS had no sense of where I stood. The clock warned me that I had only forty minutes to orient myself and get my butt to class. Looking up from my watch, I observed the flat landscape of unending sand, grass, and trees. After a pause, I knew I just needed to start moving. Finally, it hit me, and I whispered to myself, "If I can just get to the river, I can find my way back." As I moved, I scanned the horizon for a break in the treetops and looked toward the ground for wetter, darker soil. This led me through a wet prairie, and soon enough back to the marked trail. Breaking into a sprint, I scrambled back through the trail to my car, making it to class with muddy shoes, a new story, and not a minute to spare.

In just a few months (it felt like minutes), I would be rising into a new phase of my life, and I had absolutely no idea what I wanted to do. But for someone who most people identified as Type A, I felt oddly comfortable with that. The surprises and unknowns of the river had taught me to embrace the unforeseen and to use exploration as a medium for learning and reflection. By the time my final semester began, I looked optimistically at the opportunity to explore everything—from Florida's landscapes to my own personal interests and passions.

Spring (2019)

Soon enough, however, I was reminded that it's impossible to truly prepare for the unknown. I am notoriously bad at transitions. I know this about myself and made exploring and reflecting in Florida's wilderness part of my preparation for this transition. Despite all that I had learned, the spring dealt several unexpected moments that began to make my vision of post-graduation life devastatingly hazy.

Just as I was hoping to more fully invest my time and energy into wrapping up and celebrating my academic achievements, my personal relationships and values were thrown into a storm of challenges. I struggled to balance these strains in my personal life with the pending requirements of graduation. I found myself constantly crying and exhausted in efforts to be a better sister, friend, partner, student, and community member.

When exhaustion began to turn into hopelessness, a familiar thought crossed my mind—"If I can just get to the river, I can find my way back." So, I came to the river. And I kept coming back. To take a walk or to write, to do my homework, and to talk out loud. I came to the river to cry my eyes out, and I came to the river whenever I didn't know where to go. I came when I knew I needed to move from where I was but didn't know what I hoped my next step or destination would be. It served as its own point of transition.

Though I kept coming to release my thoughts and tears into the river, it didn't always have an answer. It never immediately pointed me back to my path. But to watch it snake slowly through familiar and favorite landscapes calmed me down and re-oriented me toward the peace of the present. I never got tired of watching the river. Though its movements were subtle, it showed me something new each day that I came to its refuge. In its unhurried trickle eastward, I came to see that the river was always in transition. Despite the many surrounding disturbances—rain, drought, people, traffic—it continued to flow each day, moving through each phase with grace and resilience. I made it my goal to do the same.

Summer (2019)

As I approached the sandy trailhead of the Econ River Wilderness Area, I could definitely tell that it was summer again. The path leading to the river felt new and refreshed—carpeted with a soft, bright green grass that reminded me of an Easter basket. The branches were carrying their full stock of leaves, showing off a beautiful diversity of greens in the high summer sun.

I had never seen this part of the river during the summer, but observing the fullness in the trees and the grass, I was expecting the spot to look different. When I turned down the trail to approach my favorite spot I was awestruck by what I saw. I came to an abrupt stop as I was reunited with the landscape that had become so familiar to me but now looked so different. Yes! The river did look different. It was absolutely full—its banks felt as if they were swelling with fresh water and a new flow. The field of cypress knees that I had adventured in was no longer visible, and I could not even imagine them being under the mirrored surface of the river. In that moment, I felt that I was absorbing the most beauty I ever had in my life. I let out a gasp. It felt as if the tears of the spring had transformed themselves into the fullness and renewal of summer.

Accompanying this moment of awe was a sudden flush of gratitude. From my first hike ever to this ceremonial parting hike, the river helped me rise into adulthood and showed me the values of patience, exploration, and flexibility. It taught me that there is a wide diversity of benefits in getting to know the outdoors, and that everyone can find a sense of place and belonging in our natural landscapes.

The river has affirmed to me that no matter what stage I am in life or how uncomfortable I feel in a certain space, there is something to learn and appreciate. It has given me the courage to continue embracing discomfort. The twists and turns of the spring brought me to opportunities that seemed unfathomable to me months before. Although these new adventures have to draw me away from Florida and the river for some time, I hold confidence in each new chance to learn and grow as a person. Every unknown path and breathtaking view I come across is now complemented by memories of the river, bringing me peace and focus wherever I go, no matter how many miles away.

The Breathers, St. Mark's Lighthouse

RICK CAMPBELL

I stand at the point of the oyster bar
where the water darkens and deepens,
begins to turn for the Gulf. This morning
I am early. Light is new and I think
of Mexico. Somewhere south

past clouds that ride the horizon
the Yucatan jabs into the sea.
The tide's almost slack, turning
like a man remembering his keys.

Pelicans splash like stones; snakebirds
on pilings hang their wings out to dry. Crabs
scuttle the brown shell bottom. All the fish
I do not want are alive and hungry today. Every cast
brings pinfish, needlefish, baby cat.

Dolphins tail over turtle grass beds,
roll and hump through the flats.
Water so shallow it will not cover
their broad, gray-green backs.

All four turn toward me, swim
just a few feet off the bar.
I am almost close enough to read
their minds, to put my thoughts
in their great deep eyes.

As they surface I hear them blow
and it sounds like the gasp of a runner opening his lungs to the rich air.
I listen to them, the breathers.

Where the map says Apalachee Bay,
where Narvaez sailed west in his patchwork
ships, our eyes meet; we breathe the same
air. Today, together, we are so old,
the world begins again.

PART III

ANIMALS

Birds and Refuge

FREDERICK R. DAVIS

St. Marks National Wildlife Refuge covers 68,000 acres along the Gulf Coast of the Florida Panhandle. Most tourists know it as the site of the St. Marks Lighthouse, the second oldest in Florida. Established in 1931 for the waterfowl that depended on it for safe haven, St. Marks joined a spate of depression-era refuges that significantly expanded the system of refuges in Florida and the United States. As happened at many refuges, managers directed the construction of a series of dikes to create impoundments and a road in. Many visitors never leave the air-conditioned comfort of their vehicles as they drive past a remarkable number of animals.

For me, a trip to St. Marks National Wildlife Refuge was one of the great joys of living in northern Florida for a decade and a half. From my house in Tallahassee, it was about twenty miles to the turn off to the refuge. Though wildlife sights are few and far between in the city, St. Marks always produced great views of something interesting. One trip, a family of wild pigs was rooting out on the mudflat, and on another we spotted river otters fishing along the road. Fox squirrels and bobcats occasionally appeared out of the ether momentarily, only to vanish moments later. Of course, deer and alligators were regular sightings. On one occasion a black bear stepped into view on the entrance road. My parents and I sat entranced as the bear examined roadkill. Another carload of observers slowed to a stop opposite from us. The thought occurred to me that this rare encounter would terminate when some yahoo in a pickup truck sped through the middle of our collective reverie. Just a moment later, after the bear stepped off the road, the expected truck barreled by the bear and the nature lovers.

But what drew me to St. Marks were the birds. Even in the small portion of the refuge accessible to the public, birders have reported more than three hundred avian species. The most obvious may be the waterfowl and wading birds. Every species of heron and egret appears regularly in the refuge, sometimes in scores. Duck populations expand during the winter when they migrate from places to the north. The throngs of common species of waterfowl are occasionally joined by strays from the north or the west. There is enough pine forest to host Bachman's sparrows and brown-headed nuthatches, both associated with southern forests, as well as numerous woodpeckers and common species. Given the timing of the shorebird migration, several species are generally on the move, which simply means that the dedicated birder can usually find upward of a dozen species of plovers and sandpipers, either on the flats near the lighthouse or in Tower Pond.

On a foggy or rainy day in late April, dozens of songbirds descend into the small patch of woods near Tower Pond. Sometimes up to twenty warbler species, along with vireos, orioles, tanagers, buntings, and cuckoos, flit nervously through the predominant live oaks. The occasional merlin or sharp-shinned hawk will cut through the trees in hot pursuit of a meal. Many of these birds cross the Gulf of Mexico overnight. They take off from the Yucatan Peninsula as darkness descends and fly through the night relying on fat stores and tailwinds to carry them three hundred miles or more across the Gulf. At the break of dawn, the birds can see the silhouettes of the trees, and they drop in for respite and refuge. The notion of trans-Gulf migration remained a strong hypothesis, until in 1945 Louisiana biologist George H. Lowery Jr. sailed on a freighter across the Gulf and recorded numerous songbird species migrating high overhead.

Even in the best of circumstances, the energy demands of flying hundreds of miles nonstop run high, so the birds need to refuel and recharge. Ideal conditions include southwest winds (tailwinds for northbound migrants) and clear skies so the birds can see the stars, which they use to navigate. The benefits of flying with rather than against the wind seem self-evident. Determining that the birds drew on the stars to navigate required thoughtful experiments with captive birds. E.G.F. Sauer, a German ornithologist, found that birds in a clear plexiglass cage oriented themselves toward the migratory path until clouds set in, leaving the birds confused. Subsequent tests with caged birds under the artificial night sky in a planetarium confirmed Sauer's hypothesis that migrants navigated using the stars, even when he rotated the stars of the planetarium 180 degrees.

With southwest winds and a clear sky, the small birds can cross the Gulf with energy to spare. They fly over the coastal refugia and continue on to larger tracts of forest further inland. If, on the other hand, they encounter fog or rain or adverse winds, crossing the Gulf becomes a struggle for survival as the small birds stretch the limits of their strength. Of course, optimal conditions on the Yucatan Peninsula in no way guarantee fair weather over the Gulf. When flocks of birds encounter unfavorable conditions en route, a fallout can occur as migrants "fall out" of the sky and into the trees and shrubs, even onto the beach along the coast. To witness a fallout along the Gulf is to see an extraordinary number of birds. Finding food and shelter can short-circuit the typical wariness of the survivors, affording views at unusually close range.

Barrier islands along the Gulf such as St. George Island can host spectacular fallouts with hundreds of warblers, buntings, orioles, tanagers, and many other species. The small forests at St. Marks and elsewhere serve as short stops where migrants feed and rest over the course of the day (or several days if adverse conditions persist). Yet, the point of migration is to reach breeding sites to the north.

Birds are not the only animals that stop over at St. Marks during migration. Butterflies such as Gulf fritillaries, cloudless sulfurs, and long-tailed skippers all congregate on the abundant wildflowers along the shore near the lighthouse. But it is the well-known migratory lepidopteran that attracts crowds in October: the Monarch. At times, hundreds and even thousands of Monarchs flock to St. Marks. Biologists and volunteers tag them as they rest. The refuge holds an annual festival to celebrate their arrival.

A few miles up the St. Marks River from the refuge is a nondescript dirt road, usually muddy, called Old Plank Road. It hosts a wet forest between the road and the river, and on the other side of the road is a higher forest that transitions between southern mixed hardwoods and pine forests that serves as a breeding ground for a variety of songbirds, as well as Kentucky and hooded warblers. The last were long classified in the genus *Wilsonia*, named for the great nineteenth-century American ornithologist Alexander Wilson. Wilson's biographical details indicate that he knew many renowned naturalists in America during the years of the early republic, including Audubon, who he convinced to devote himself to painting. Like Audubon, Wilson painted the birds of North America. In mid-May, the breeding songs of several hooded warblers on the territory ring out along Bottoms Road, and occasionally a Kentucky warbler will disclose its location with its more lyrical song. If I missed Kentuckys during the migration, I was confident I could find them again along Old Plank Road.

The wet cypress swamp on the riverine side of the road even hosted a Swainson's warbler on occasion. Unlike the striking yellow, green, and black plumage of both hooded warblers and Kentuckys, the plumage of the Swainson's is a study in earth tones: brown and olive with a rufous crown. Most birders become familiar with the haunting whistled song of the Swainson's long before they see one. I did actually see the bird itself on several occasions along Old Plank Road. After about three miles, state-owned and managed pine plantations predominate, and the number of birds drops off precipitously, but the first three miles are a treasure, a remnant of the forest that once covered large swaths along the rivers of Florida.

A few years ago, I drove the twenty or so miles from my house to Old Plank Road. It was already the middle of May, so rather than continuing on to St. Marks I turned directly onto Old Plank Road. The imminent sight of uncommon warblers had me completely preoccupied, so I was utterly unprepared for the view that greeted me as I proceeded down the road. The trees had vanished. Where the thin strip of riverine Cypress forest had stood the year before were now lot lines indicated by surveyors' stakes. I was amazed at how close the road was to the river. No houses or docks had been constructed: all that remained were completely cleared lots, each identical to the ones adjacent. About three miles down, the state-managed forest began. The only sounds were from the occasional northern Parula. The Kentucky and Swainson's warblers had disappeared with the habitat. It goes without saying that most of the other birds are also gone. I turned around and drove out. Several years have passed, and there are no signs of the planned development, assuming Google maps is a good guide. Where southern mixed hardwoods stood, palmettos and other Florida scrub plants have appeared.

I have not returned to Old Plank Road, but the thought occurred to me that I finally understood why the great sea turtle biologist Archie Carr struggled to complete a book about Florida. Over the course of more than fifty years, Carr witnessed the disappearance of countless swamps and lakes and forests of every type. Most distressing to the person who determined the importance of Florida beaches to nesting loggerhead and green sea turtles was the rampant and extensive beach development. Marjorie Harris Carr, a wildlife scientist married to Archie, famously organized the fight to save the Ocklawaha River from the ambitions of the Army Corps of Engineers to build the Cross-Florida

Barge Canal, one of the great achievements for Florida conservationists. But the Carrs saw many ecosystems vanish as well. I suppose I should consider myself fortunate to witness the demise of only one small patch of prime habitat.

Happily, the presence of St. Marks National Wildlife Refuge running along the Gulf Coast offers some reassurance. Management of refuges now privileges habitat for wildlife over hunting and fishing, which bodes well for the continued presence of birds and other animals there. In her book *Refuge*, Terry Tempest Williams explores the meanings of wildlife refuge as a safe haven for birds, and also as a setting where she finds rejuvenation in the face of the breast cancer ravaging her mother, her sister, and herself. The refuge metaphor succeeds on multiple levels, and speaks to those of us who seek birds and solace in settings such as St. Marks. A refuge for birds and wildlife also provides a refuge for us.

The Quiet Song of Sanibel Island

CYNTHIA BARNETT

To hear the ocean's softest song, walk the southern beaches of Sanibel Island. Listen closely at the break line. As each wave pulls back to sea, a sparkly tinkle rises from the rumble. It's the jingle of tiny shells. They ring from the quietest side of the aural spectrum, place of fairy-dust notes and first rains.

Lying off Fort Myers Beach in southwest Florida, Sanibel is not a metaphor for seashells, but a synonym. The island's land mass, itself, was formed out of "innumerable millions of shells, their reduction to fragments, and finally to shell sand," as the Field Museum malacologist Fritz Haas wrote in 1940. "The beach represents a vast mortuary."

Most of Florida's 4,500 barrier islands run north and south in parallel to the mainland. Sanibel juts sidelong, terminus of a band of Gulf of Mexico currents that heaped the shells, fragments, and sand over the past five thousand years. It lies east to west in a wide, upturned curve, shaped like the Cheshire Cat's smile. As mollusks and their shells tumble along in the Gulf's tides, currents, and storms, the animals and their coveted homes are trapped by twelve miles of beach sloping gently along the cat's chin.

For shell lovers, every tide brings a treasure hunt. At water's edge, the tinkling slurry of wee clams, cockles, and coquinas, augers and tritons, drills and murex, opaque jingles, and other miniatures paves the landing for the larger bounty: horse conchs and crown conchs. Tapered lightning whelks and their twisty crepe-paper egg casings. Tulip shells and turban shells. Sand dollars that cover your palm, and starfish big as dinner plates. And those are just the commoners among more than three hundred Gulf and Caribbean species that wash ashore.

At low tide, the shoreline is a mosaic of rippling flats, the toe-tickling shell slurry, tide pools, and lagoons. It's also full of life, slight to the eye. Kneel to the wet-sand world of a Florida fighting conch, shell polished deep brown and orange. Protruding from two notches at the tip of its shell, two curious eye stalks periscope the scene. Coast apparently clear, the animal stretches its soft pink body onto the squishy sand and uses its nimble foot to tai chi toward the sea.

For a century, collectors have scoured the shore before dawn for prize shells, less interested in the mollusks within. Headlamps shining in the dark, the methodically sweeping figures can look eerily like an amphibious invasion. But those shell-soldiers miss what makes Sanibel Island exceptional. It's not Haas's vast mortuary or the empty shells of dead mollusks. It's the quiet, slow-moving world of living ones.

. . .

Despite childhood summers spent on infinite Florida beaches with two patient grandmothers to admire shells and press them into bucket sand castles, my life's searing memory of seashells is heavy with the contents of another plastic bucket, one of my late father's.

Before either was fashionable, Russell Rousseau Barnett was a forager of useful items discarded by others, and also wild foods. He kept a stash of white five-gallon buckets he picked up regularly from a Tampa food distributor, and used them for everything. He'd take them camping to stow gear, fill them with kindling, then turn them upside down for campfire stools.

Happiest roaming in the woods or waters of his native Florida, his formal name never fit; my father was always Rusty. Likewise, his forest and sea adventures were never patrician. Every camping trip was epic, not infrequently with a late-night brandishing of his pistol to protect us from threats that only he could see.

The ocean sang to Rusty, too, but in the blare of a conch trumpet rather than the chime of tiny shells. On one father-daughter trip to Key West, count: one pistol wielded at an invisible enemy; one boat broken down offshore at dusk; one ER visit to treat him for swarming man-o-war stings; one partial victory fending off a pervert on Duval Street while Rusty spent the evening at the bar at Sloppy Joe's; a fuller victory shaking Rusty awake at midnight to evacuate a motel fire. On the same trip, my father taught me to spearfish, and told me the Mayan legend of the kapok tree: how the souls of the dead ascend its branches to heaven.

No vacation was more memorable. But with my father, even a day-trip on his boat had to be a mission, say, to watch the sun rise and set on the same day—or to collect enough conchs for a homemade pot of chowder.

When I was fifteen, we spent a winter day hopping sandbars and barrier islands in southwest Florida to fill one of his ubiquitous five-gallon buckets with live whelks and conchs. Imagining how the shells might brighten his bachelor-neglected flowerbeds on Chelsea Street in Tampa, I was caught up.

Rusty's philosophy was that it was okay to hook, spear, or otherwise gather marine life as long as we ate it. Back in his kitchen, I saw that I'd gathered more conchs than we could eat, including Florida fighting conchs for their polished brown and orange shells. He followed the recipe from Irma Rombauer's *Joy of Cooking*: cover the conchs with cold water, simmer twenty to thirty minutes, remove from the shell "and beat the white body meat in a canvas bag until it begins to disintegrate."

The "removing" was more agony than joy, and hardly worth it for the conchs' little pink bodies. Still, Rusty pried them out with his pocketknife, made an enormous, over-spiced pot of conch chowder, and declared it sublime.

I didn't share the sentiment. The wasted lives weighed on me as long as he lived on Chelsea Street, as the brown-and-orange shells I pressed into the flowerbeds were soon crushed, buried, or swept away in the Florida rain.

. . .

In the first edition of her classic *Shell Book*, published in 1908, the seashell-writer Julia Ellen Rogers was already lamenting the rising tide of visitors descending on Sanibel Island, and their daily hoarding of all the best specimens. "Sanibel is too popular," she wrote. "Too faithfully are her beaches scanned."

In 1921, William J. ("Bill") Clench, then a young field biologist, took his second shell-collecting trip to Sanibel and found a bounty of miniature specimens such as pointy augers and coquinas along the beach and fronting Sanibel's iron tower lighthouse. Yet it was a disappointing haul compared with the past. "Many shells formerly common on Sanibel have disappeared, while others have become quite rare," he wrote. "The abundance of shells on the island, especially the larger and more showy species, attracts many tourist-collectors during the winter season. . . . This might in part explain the paucity of many of these forms that were abundant a few years ago."

Still, by 1927 it was clear that Sanibel would hitch its fortunes to seashells. That year, as Florida began to spiral in its first real estate bust, the island hosted the first Sanibel Shell Show as a financial and psychological lift.

While the rest of the state beat the nation to the Great Depression, seashells kept Sanibel from scraping the economic bottom. The 1930s saw the first sustained national media coverage of the island's polished attractions, and of shell collecting as a growing hobby. News stories described two knee-deep windrows of shells paralleling the beaches, replenished on the high tides. The *Christian Science Monitor* described how professional harvesters and collectors alike crawled the rows before dawn to pick up "anything new." Commercial shellers hired workers to sweep the beaches, and to dredge for live specimens out in the Gulf of Mexico.

In a scornful article, the novelist Theodore Pratt described in the *Saturday Evening Post* what by 1940 had become standard in every seaside motel: special boiling stations to encourage tourists to kill and clean their mollusks down by the beach instead of in their rooms. So many pots boiling at once, "so that the mollusks may be removed from their shells without a tug-of-war," created a hellacious stench in the Sanibel night air.

The nation was becoming "shell shocked," Pratt wrote. "Shell collecting is now one of the major attractions for souvenir-hunting visitors to the orange-blossom-state," gushed a 1952 story in the *New York Times*. Reporting from southwest Florida a few years later, the *Washington Post* called shell-collecting "the nation's fastest-growing hobby." The writer added the collecting ethos of the day: "Real shell collectors must take a shell alive in order to have it count, just the way bird watchers may not score birds observed in captivity, heaven forfend."

Pratt told the story of an amateur collector who drove down from Chicago so he could load his car trunk with shells. On the trip back home, he called for his car at the hotel garage where he'd left it overnight and was seized by the police, who'd been called to investigate the stink. When they opened the trunk, the cops found not one dead body, as hotel employees had suspected, but thousands.

• • •

The most varied of all the earth's animals, mollusks are beings that peer back at us through two retractable eyes mounted at the tip of waving tentacles, or a hundred electric blue eyes set in dazzling rows. They are creatures with rapacious tongues and rows of teeth to feed their big, wolf-hungry stomachs. They are animals that dive and leap. They are animals that scurry across the ocean floor, burrow into sand, climb up rocks, turn corners, and flip somersaults. Animals that leave tracks clear as racoon paws in mud. Animals that swim—propelled forward by wings graceful as butterflies, or backward by clapping shells. Animals that ascend and descend in the water column—some regulating themselves with chambers they fill with gas like a master diver who perfected buoyancy over 400 million years.

They are animals that breathe and bleed and have a beating heart. Yet our infatuation with them is generally caught only after the beating heart has stopped.

Twenty-five years ago, Sanibel Island set out to change that ethos. The community that tied its fortunes to nature's unrivaled architectural works took a stand to protect the animal-architects, themselves. In 1994, Sanibel became the first city in the United States to ban live shelling. At first, the ban bitterly divided the town and its shell lovers. The world's leading malacologist, then working to found the first national shell museum on Sanibel, ridiculed the proposal as "screwy" and "extreme."

Today, the Bailey-Matthews National Shell Museum leads a new ethic in the human relationship with mollusks. Its volunteer "Shell Ambassadors" walk the southern beaches and answer tourists' questions about shells and the lives of the animals that build them. The museum has opened the world's first aquarium devoted solely to live mollusks. At a big touch tank, kids can watch a moon snail bury itself in the sand for protection, or peer into the curious eyes of a Florida fighting conch.

I was at the touch tank with my teenaged son and daughter, all of us mesmerized by a fighting conch's periscoping eyes, when Rusty's bucket of conchs and whelks washed over me. A dreadlocked marine scientist named Rebecca Mensch told us the burly brown-and-orange conchs that once filled beachfront boiling pots are the most ill-named of all the mollusks. They were christened by an eighteenth-century scientist who never observed the live animal, but imagined its shell a Medieval mace. Far from fighters, the creatures are the gentlest of vegetarians.

. . .

I recently returned to Key West and walked around where Rusty and I had our epic adventures and misadventures nearly four decades ago. Long before, he'd left his 1920s bachelor's bungalow on Chelsea Street in Tampa for a Cracker house he built deep in the southwest Florida pine scrub. One year before, he'd died alone there.

A conch-shell trumpet still blared in tourist-packed Mallory Square, the ocean's loudest song. Duval Street was disorienting for me. Passing a Gap Factory Store and Banana Republic, I could have been in any number of American cities—including Waikiki Beach in Honolulu, which has similarly corporatized its once-singular Kalakaua Avenue, now home to a Margaritaville. Rusty would have been scandalized.

How Sanibel could preserve its quiet sea song amid the pressure to build Margaritaville chains from here to Niagara Falls is a tale much bigger than the living mollusks the island now celebrates. Even in its midcentury shell-collecting heyday, the existential threat was never that Sanibel would run out of shells—but that it would be run over with the coastal development filling Florida's wetlands, felling its mangrove forests, flattening its dunes, and erecting pink condo towers to block pink sunsets.

Sanibel's leaders had the vision, and the courage, to do the two things that mattered most: They planned long-term to balance ecological preservation and growth, passing the Sanibel Plan in the 1970s to ensure new development would never overrun the nature that defined the place. And they preserved 67 percent of the island as conservation land, protecting not only beaches, but the vast estuaries, backwaters, and Calusa shell mounds that give Sanibel its feel of civilized wild. The Sanibel-Captiva Conservation Foundation manages more than twelve hundred acres of coastline, interior freshwaters, and forests. The J. N. "Ding" Darling National Wildlife Refuge preserves upward of five thousand more, including a dark, watery woodland that stands as the largest undeveloped mangrove ecosystem left in the United States.

Like the shift from boiling mollusks alive to celebrating their lives, Sanibel's conservation ethic evolved over time. Developers had built roads and filled wetlands along the Sanibel River for twelve hundred homes. Today, those wetlands and the river's oxbows are restored. No garish pink high rises block Sanibel's searing pink sunsets. There are no billboards, or outlandish signs of any kind. Fast-food and chain restaurants are banned.

The motels have kept their midcentury motor court charm, but not their killing stations. Tide charts are stamped with reminders to take only empty shells. At the Island Inn's shell-cleaning station—now just a big sink—a cartoon gastropod in flip flops reminds visitors: "Don't take us home if we are still alive!"

Exclusivity has brought its own set of problems. On my latest visit, I stopped in at a beach shop when I saw out of the corner of my eye a familiar five-gallon bucket, white and plastic like Rusty's old catchalls and fireside seats, but with a brand name. I flipped the price tag, $49.99. Lid sold separately, $29.99. I had a belly laugh with my late father—just like him, seeing someone who wasn't there.

The Habits of Alligators (1993)

LOREN G. "TOTCH" BROWN

Alligators don't like saltwater. In the dry season as the water in the islands and rivers becomes salty, the gators swim upriver to the Glades. Instead of crawling they get up on all fours and walk out into the Glades looking for freshwater, and also a place to hibernate through the dry season. Some find a low place and dig their own hole down to the freshwater, while others prefer something like a small lake ditch. After hibernation is over (around June or July) and the rains come again, back down the little rivers lickety-split they go, eating everything they can grab. Their habitat changes from the islands in rainy season to a hole in the dried-up Everglades in the dry season. And I mean *dry*, since as we know some stupid politicians managed to get it all diked off.

Gators make three distinct sounds. One is the "grunt" used by young gators in distress to call their mothers. When you pick up a baby gator, it'll start "grunting" every time. The mother will respond to this sound right away. (With practice, you can imitate this "grunt" and often fool a grown gator into coming to you.)

Then there's the blowing sound gators make when they're more or less hemmed up, or concerned, and are good and mad.

The third sound is the gator bellow—a bloodcurdling sound that can be heard for miles across the Everglades. When one gator bellows, another will usually answer. When the big boar gators are bellowing in the deep stillness of the night and you're out in the bushes alone with all the other weird animal sounds (maybe a Florida panther scream or two), you start looking around to see what's coming out next.

When a twelve-foot gator bellows, he raises his head up as high as possible, his mouth wide open, and with a full breath, lets out his air. It's a sight to be seen (and a sound to be heard)! The bellowing is generally in mating season, the late spring, when the rains are about to start. The gators seem to be asking Mother Nature for a drink of water.

Oh, and there's a fourth sound. A wounded gator makes a goggling sound, and that gator is something to be scared of when you're in a pit pan.[*] One night, Peg[†] and I were hunting in Little Fox Lake, north of Flamingo, in a pit pan with very little freeboard (freeboard is the amount of space between the waterline and the top of the boat.) Peg was doing the shooting with a common .22-caliber rifle.

The water was a little rough that night, making it hard even for a pro like Peg to knock out a gator every time. When he shot one eight-footer, it wasn't a fatal shot. The gator started running around on top of the water with his mouth wide open. Soon he headed straight into the front end of our pan, into Peg's lap. When Peg tried to shove the gator away, he ended up with his whole arm in the gator's mouth. By a miracle, the gator didn't clamp down and Peg was able to pull his arm back, torn up a bit.

While this was going on, I was trying to keep the boar from turning over. By the time Peg shoved the gator out of the boat, there was so much water in it we didn't dare move a finger. An empty milk can was floating around in the pan, but we were so near sinking neither of us could make a move to get it. Finally, by paddling careful with my hand, I got ahold of the can and bailed her out.

---

[*]   A flat-bottom boat used for hunting alligators.
[†]   Totch's older brother Melvin.

Gator!

LEE IRBY

"Gator!" the children cry. The word floats up into the canopy of the pine hammock before it crashes down onto the trail where I'm walking. The kids feel comfortable at Boyd Hill Nature Preserve, a 245-acre oasis amid the bustle of Pinellas, the most urbanized county in Florida. They've more or less grown up here, frolicking on the playground, exploring the scrub, chasing after snakes in the flatwoods . . .

But there's always one overarching goal: to see an alligator. A trip to Boyd Hill without seeing a gator is a disappointment that happens frequently in the summer, when gators sink to the bottom of Lake Maggiore to stay cool. But this is January, when Florida's herpetological fauna come to life.

The kids have run ahead of us and then rounded a corner toward Wax Myrtle Pond. We, Justyna and I, can't see them, only hear the word that captures the wild heart of Florida like no other. "Gator!" Justyna was born in Poland, raised in New York City . . . her experience with the natural landscape of Florida pretty much consisted of our walks through Boyd Hill, which she did with some reluctance because of her fear of alligators. I assured her that she had nothing to worry about, and the saurians we did see were either the young of the year basking on a sunny bank or, from a safe distance, an adult swimming through the murk.

Facts (sort of) confirm my bland promise to Justyna, that no alligator would ever harm her children, nor mine. According to the Florida Fish and Wildlife Commission, since 1948 there have been twenty-five fatal alligator bites out of 282 major attacks. Although the state is home to 1.25 million alligators, the chance of a person being killed by one is remote, 1 in 2.4 million. From a statistical standpoint, it was far more dangerous for us to drive to the nature park (chance of dying: one in 29,627) than to walk in it.

But we're not walking anymore. The yell "gator!" acts as a catalyst, turning our leisurely stroll into a panicked gallop. Our kids range in age from seven to three, not old enough to handle the situation. My children have seen alligators aplenty, so for them to cry out the word . . . this is no ordinary gator. Like French artist and explorer Jacques le Moyne, I can imagine a beast of twenty feet or more, an absolute giant of a creature. The largest alligator ever recorded in Florida measured over seventeen feet; le Moyne's engravings from the 1500s are not exaggerations.

Actuarial tables and historical drawings mean nothing to us now. Justyna's silence speaks volumes: she assumes the worst. Logic and reason retreat when an ancient life form intrudes and reduces existence to that eternal struggle of avoiding predation. Modern Florida has tried to remove the cold, hard battle that defined hominid life for countless generations. But despite the best efforts of Walt Disney and Henry Flagler, Florida remains a place where humans are on the menu.

Mothers in Manhattan worry about child abduction, not child ingestion. The worst thing that can happen in a New York nature park is perhaps a bear sighting. Parents in most states don't envision their little ones being devoured—and neither do the tourists who come here on vacation. Sadly, the dreamscape created by Walt's imaginers have had tragic consequences. In June 2016, the world recoiled in horror when Lane Graves, a two-year-old visiting from Nebraska, while playing in the shallow water of the Seven Seas Lagoon, was dragged away by an alligator.

No one who studies the ecosystems of Florida was very surprised. Despite its name, the Seven Seas Lagoon is a humanmade body of freshwater in Central Florida, where the fossil record for alligators extends back several million years. Morphologically, these reptiles have changed very little over time. They are opportunistic feeders, and mostly hunt and eat vertebrates, especially fish. If anything can define the wild heart of Florida, it is the tableau of an alligator's snout barely above the surface of the water, gliding silently in search of prey.

But Walt Disney, along with countless other developers in Florida, thought the Sunshine State could be tamed, and in taming the land, rid the citizens of the dread, the fear, the horror, of an alligator attack. At water's edge, around nine o'clock in the evening, little Lane was building sand castles without a care in the world. A No Swimming sign was posted but no specific warning about alligators. Trappers had removed forty gators from Disney property during the previous twelve months, but there was no reason to suspect that within the manufactured paradise that is Walt Disney World a fundamental collision would occur between an unwitting vertebrate and a hungry reptile.

Old-timers know not to splash around in a Florida lake at night. In 2004, Michelle Reeves came to Fort Myers on a college break to visit her grandparents. They warned her not to swim in the retention pond by the house, but sometime during the night Michelle ignored the admonition and went skinny-dipping. Her nightgown was found on the bank, and her arm was found inside an eight-foot gator.

Even so, attacks are quite rare. Alligators have a natural aversion to humans, another reason I respect these animals. Yes, the statistics bolstered the promise I made to Justyna, but when I made the assurance, a study had yet to be performed that would reframe my declaration of safe passage through Boyd Hill. In 2018, biologists at the University of North Florida tried to determine why the incidence of alligator attack was rising, from an average of one every three years between 1988 and 1999 to seven per year since then. Their conclusion: the only variable that accounts for the increase is a concomitant surge in human-alligator interactions.

In other words, alligators were attacking people more often in Florida because more people were living here than ever before, moving into alligator habitat and encountering the reptiles at a greater rate. Of course, as I hurry down the trail with Justyna, I'm ignorant of this finding, just as Lane's parents didn't know to be watchful while near freshwater. Lane's father tried to save his son but couldn't wrestle the child from the gator's maw. After a struggle, the gator disappeared into the black water with its prey, and Lane's parents and Disney staff and local law enforcement did everything they could to find Lane.

Find him they did, the next day. He'd been drowned, not eaten. Five gators were captured and destroyed, and wildlife officials were confident but not positive that the round-up in fact netted the culprit. Disney called in trappers in an attempt to cleanse the grounds of alligators, and quickly signs and chains and ropes sprang up along every canal, lake, fishing hole, and sluice on Disney property. Snakes were also implicated in the Disney warnings, but in my dozens of visits, I'd only ever seen a black racer, a nonvenomous species, by Typhoon Lagoon. In one fell swoop, Disney went from salutary neglect to a Hitchcock movie on steroids, where all animals were potential killers.

Boyd Hill has signs posted throughout the park, warning visitors that it's illegal to feed or molest alligators, that swimming in the ponds isn't allowed, that you have entered wild country, even though the hum of the city isn't far away. The entire point of places like Boyd Hill is that those who need solace from civilization can find it amid the native flora and fauna. Many of my Eckerd College students have spent hours here removing invasive air potato and Brazilian pepper, and I can see their restoration efforts taking root right before my eyes.

But even this version of nature is socially constructed. So many of us badly want for nature to be "re-wilded," returned to its pristine state, but without carefully considering whether our vision is in fact ecologically accurate. Humans have disturbed landscapes for millennia, and thus our repairs are often as artificial as the disturbance we seek to remedy. Regardless of our intentions, one thing that restoration ecologists can count on is that alligators are native to freshwater ecosystems in Florida. This isn't social construction, this isn't discourse that reifies stereotypes, this isn't the febrile dreams of flower children—no, this is the central reality of Florida, that gators dominate as an apex predator, and no postmodernist can quibble with that assertion.

Right now, our children are within arm's reach of an apex predator. It takes us only a minute to catch up to them. When we turn the corner toward the pond, we see the four of them, two blond boys of three, two brunette girls of seven, huddled together beneath a cabbage palm. It's a chilly day in January—a cold front has pulled through, leaving behind a bright sun. A ten-foot gator has taken the opportunity to warm itself in a bright spot along the bank of the pond.

My son, a budding field biologist, is standing perhaps two feet away from jaws that look to be about his size. In all my years of tromping around Florida, I've never seen a bigger alligator, from a distance or this close. The beast doesn't move a muscle, but instead conserves its energy and lets the rays of the sun elevate its body temperature. Our lives, our hopes and dreams, our vision of nature as garden or wilderness, sublime or savage, mean nothing to this reptile. If it had been hungry, it would have taken my son into the pond and gone into a death roll to drown him. Since 1948, twenty-five other humans have met this same fate, including four children around my son's age, such as Lane Graves.

I think a lot about Lane's father, who literally fought an alligator to save his son—and lost. He told authorities that he reached into the alligator's mouth and grabbed its teeth in an effort to free Lane, but the saurian was so powerful that with one whip of the tail, it vanished, with Lane in tow. That kind of primitive showdown, with the fate of a child hanging in the balance, taking place in the shadow of Cinderella's castle, captures the complexity of wild Florida. The changes have come so furiously, and yet parts will forever elude the grasp of the rapacious despoilers.

Calmly, I lead my son away from the alligator, alert for any sudden movements. There are none. Alligators are ambush hunters and strike when defenses are down. They are more active in warm weather and can go years without eating. The alligator that trappers think attacked Lane had an empty stomach.

Justifiably, Justyna is a little upset. I'd promised her that alligators weren't a danger, and yet our children came incredibly close to . . . to what? Not to dying, because nothing happened. They came close to something ineffable, irreducible, and ineluctable—to life as it was when dinosaurs roamed the earth and proto-mammals scurried in the darkness. These same mammals would eventually spawn the greatest killer of all-time, a killer who by the 1960s would reduce the alligator population to a few thousand.

But this same killer would pass laws to protect the dwindling reptiles, and so the killer stopped killing and alligators recovered, a conservation success story. Florida was "re-wilded" even as it was denuded and pillaged. Preservation and destruction: the two simultaneous trajectories Florida has unevenly followed.

To her credit, Justyna continued to go on nature walks with me, but she preferred the boardwalks of Weedon Island. Alligators don't do well in saltwater. Crocodiles, however, can live in brackish or saltwater areas. I never told her one was spotted in our county.

Feast of Pythons (Homage to Harry Crews)

ISAAC EGER

I asked, *How'll I know when I see one?*

Somewhere deep in the Everglades I pointed the spotlight at the night ahead of the truck that carried us along the crushed limestone path of Levee 28.

It's just one of those things you'll know when you see it, they said.

The levee's road ran so straight for so long that the light got gobbled up by all the dark and looked like it might go on forever. I pointed the light back to the levee's banks, looking for something that wasn't supposed to be there. We were python hunting. Trying to make Florida natural again.

The truck belonged to a real Florida boy, some generations deep, whose name, I shit you not, is Dusty Crum. Dusty's a famous python hunter now. He's got his own TV show, except on the show they usually hunt during the day and on foot. But the snakes are most active at night. When all the other critters are out. There weren't any other critters tonight but for an occasional palm rat. The snakes had eaten most everything else.

Dusty's thirty-eight years old, but you might confuse him for someone much older. Not because he looks old—though he's got a lot of gray in his beard and long hair that falls under a dirty baseball cap—but because he looks like he belongs to the land, and the land in Florida seems ancient, like something the dinosaurs might have enjoyed.

I asked, *How many snakes you reckon are out here?*

A lot, Dusty said. *Hundreds of thousands.*

Nowhere on earth do invasive species thrive like they do in Florida. It only took about twenty years for these pythons to eat damn near everything and usurp gators as the apex killer. Native species don't stand a chance.

I, too, am a Florida native—a fact I've begun to parade around now that Florida is literary hot shit. A fact that might not seem so meaningful since this is my first time actually setting foot in the Everglades. I'd driven through it, many times, on that eighty-mile-long concrete lesion we call Alligator Alley. But I'm here, tryin' to get my bona fides, hunting invasive Burmese python, tryin' to save what's left of what Florida's supposed to be because the Florida I grew up in turns out to be a counterfeit.

Florida is a strange land full of strangers. When I was young it was the tourists who were the foreigners, and all the little precious creatures I loved from my childhood, these things that I believed were here before we had a name for anything, were true Florida nature. Then I'd learn that I'd loved invaders. Unwelcome nature that escaped our stewardship and made a home out of our state. Feels like I can no longer look back fondly at my memories as a boy catching lizards in my folks' backyard. It seemed so wild back then. Like something that all children did throughout time. But these were brown anoles from Cuba and didn't belong in southwest Florida. Same goes for the beaches lined with Australian pines that got too close to the water and became petrified with salt to create a spindly forest. Those tadpoles I'd gather after a hard rain, fed lettuce, mourned the little ones who never got to grow legs, released the survivors back into the wild—those were Cuban tree frogs that swallowed our smaller native species whole. The once beloved things of my childhood I must reimagine as marauding aliens, corrupting the balance of what was supposed to be.

So here I am. Making up for it. Making Florida natural again.

Dusty's girlfriend Natalie drove the truck. She chain-smoked Marlboro Golds while a beagle with a red bandana 'round its neck named Riley sat shotgun. The truck ambled just fast enough so that the bugs didn't bother us. You could still see them flyin' all around from the glow of the vehicle. The bugs turned white in the light we created and looked like a flurry of snow that didn't know which way to fall. I sat in a chair propped up high in the middle of the bed of the truck. A long metal slat crossed the back of the truck so that two others could hang off either side and watch both the levee banks and quickly hop off if a python got spotted. Dusty was on the left, and his friend Gregory sat on the right.

Back up, back up! Dusty shouted at Natalie and hit the roof of the truck with the flat of his palm.

The truck reversed. It was nothing. A fallen branch. Natalie put the truck back into drive.

The pythons come up on the dry banks of the levee to lay eggs and hunt, Dusty explained.

Dusty learned that from firsthand experience—he ain't no biologist. He's only been hunting pythons since 2012 when a TV show sponsored a python removal competition. Dusty and his friends have taken it upon themselves to save the Everglades. Before they got state permission to patrol the levee, they'd ride their bikes up and down the levee during the midday summer heat. The snakes they'd caught would be too heavy—sometimes over a hundred pounds—to carry all at once, so they'd have to go back and forth, carrying maybe one at a time.

Now Dusty better knows the trade, and we chatted about the business end of things. How he might be able to turn a profit out of this endeavor of his. He's skinning the snakes, turning their scaly hide into leather. Eating the meat. A Cambodian neighbor is turning the guts into some kind of traditional anti-arthritic medicine. But the Asian market makes these snake pelts for pennies on the dollar, fattening them up in cages on snake farms like some kind of cold-blooded veal. It'd be hard to imagine Dusty a rich man anyway. Always says he's doing this for the land and not a buck. I believe him because he's not cruel.

Dusty said, *It ain't their fault. They're beautiful creatures just doing what God created 'em to do. It's not like I got anythin' personal against 'em. I just care more about our native future.*

They have to kill 'em when they catch 'em. Used to be that he'd bring the snakes back to the Florida Fish and Wildlife Conservation officials and they'd euthanize the pythons. Now he's gotta kill 'em in the field unless he runs into someone else who will do it for him. There's a dime-sized kill spot on the top of their skull. A .22 rifle does it.

It's sad killing the little ones right when they hatch. They're kinda cute, Dusty said.

Besides the battery-powered spotlights in our hands, a bar of LED lights about two feet long was hooked to loose wires that led back to the engine of the truck.

That's some hucklebuck shit there, boy. That's how Dusty described his electrical set up. *Gotta make do with what you got,* he clarified. A lot of his truck he called *hucklebuck,* which is Floridian for jerry-rigged.

Not long into the journey down Levee 28, the lights died. Dusty and Greg popped the hood and peered into the smoking engine.

Fuse is all fucked up, said Greg.

You done sabotaged me, son, Dusty said, only sorta joking.

The moon swung just above our heads to the left, and the bugs started to land on us and taste our skin. The light rested in the bottom third of the moon like it was a bowl filled with white water.

That means there are lots of fish ready to bite, Greg told me. *And when the moon is gone, the snakes will come out.* He smiled.

There was a lot of optimism about this hunt.

The lights came back and the truck went on.

It was hard to tell how much time had passed. So much of the Everglades was the same. A thick green loop interrupted only by the occasional dead amber of a fallen tree.

There were many sounds. Buzzing and clicking. Heavy drones and distant yelps. Sounds of things I didn't know belonged to what. I thought of all the things I didn't know the name of. I knew the Burmese python, though. Why didn't they evolve here if it serves them so well? It makes survival of the fittest seem inaccurate somehow. You can't be too fit, I thought. Irony is the Burmese python is threatened in its native habitat.

Never bothered to ask Dusty about politics. He wore a *Don't Tread on Me* hat, and that could mean a few things. Conservation is conservative. I suppose when you live near the land you're gonna feel it change first. Florida is changing, *is* changed. Dusty is trying to slow that change. But if you ask him if it's possible to rid Florida of the pythons, he won't kid you. The snakes are here to stay, are a part of Florida for however long Florida will be. News programs end their segments about Dusty with that affected cadence: *These pythons . . . may have finally . . . met their match.* But it's only an act of God that could return the land. So fighting these snakes becomes symbolic. It's a tangible opponent. The changing world is something beyond touch. You can't be outside of a system and hold it while it holds you. But you can grab these snakes behind the mandible and drag them out of the world.

The truck veered off to the right. Natalie had fallen asleep. The three of us gave a holler and slapped the truck. We went down the embankment. I readied myself to abandon ship. She hit the brakes, and the truck stopped and then teetered. Fortunately, it wasn't a particularly steep incline. If we had flipped, Greg would have been a goner. We got the truck out and back onto the road.

There's something uncomfortably familiar about the fervor behind hunting invasive species. I'd hunted lionfish before—another invader menacing the waters of Florida. I'd killed them with a sense of righteousness. *Fish, I am obligated to shove this spear through your face.* I'd always felt bad about killing anything—even a fish—but because I was told this was a wicked fish, killing it was good and felt good. A promotional poster for the 2019 Tampa Bay Spearfishing Challenge crossed my social media feed. Underneath an illustration of the Skyway Bridge is an excessively muscular merman with familiar blond hair in front of a wall. He's pointing a gun at a spooked lionfish. The guy who posted the picture wrote: *This is my new favorite depiction of my America. Merman Trump defending the wall with his Glock.*

It was after four in the morning, and we hadn't found anything. Everyone seemed disappointed—probably on my behalf. They wanted me to see the problem for myself. It seemed odd wishing to see the thing. Wasn't it better that they weren't there? But they are there. As a sort of consolation, Dusty pulled out the fifteen-footer he'd caught the night before. The snake sat in a bag—I think it was a pillowcase. Dusty pulled it out of a compartment attached to the side of his truck. I expected him to flop the thing out on to the ground the way you would a sack of trash, but he was very gentle. The snake was out and seemed to know it should escape, but it didn't move with great desperation. She was beautiful. There was a hidden symmetry to the skin that my mind couldn't quite figure out. Dusty told me to grab her by the back of the head, but not to grip her to death. He draped the snake over my shoulders. She was heavy. She felt waxy and cool in my hands like she was impervious to the humidity. She was docile. Like she had given up, knew her fate, and was at peace with that. Dusty took pictures of me for me to show my friends.

The Florida we are trying to preserve is the Florida that serves us. I wondered what made me any more Floridian than this snake in my arms. Because I was born here? I thought about oranges. They ain't from here, neither. The Spanish brought them here from Europe, and the Portuguese brought them there from China five hundred years ago. Now they're on our license plates. We brought her here and now we are trying to get rid of her. She's just doing the only thing she knows how. It crossed my mind that I should let her go.

One Manatee, Two Nations

ANMARI ALVAREZ ALEMÁN

It was the winter of 2007. I had recently graduated from the University of Havana with a degree in biology when I received a call from a powerplant official forty miles away in North Havana. Two manatees had been found inside the plant's intake canal. He was looking for a biologist who could see if they were okay. It was late in the day, and I didn't have a car. I decided to hitchhike to the powerplant.

When I got there, I was asked for my identification and given a helmet. I walked through what felt like the ruins of an old and rusty factory, kept cranking with the sheer ingenuity of the Cuban people. Then I saw them, a mother manatee with her calf, resting peacefully in a small canal. They looked powerful, majestic—and incredibly vulnerable.

Seeing a wild Cuban manatee for the first time filled me with joy. That moment solidified my career choice: to research manatee biology and help these creatures survive the age of humans.

The surprise came weeks later when I realized that it wasn't a Cuban but a Florida manatee that first inspired my career decision. The mother was covered in scars. Caused by propellers, the scars suggested she wasn't from Cuba, where the seas are largely silent of the buzz of boat motors so familiar in Florida. She was indeed known and registered in Florida, by the code CR131, since 1979. In Cuba, she'd been named "Daysi" by the powerplant workers, who to my surprise, were really excited by the visit of such interesting characters. Before arriving in Havana, Daysi had last been sighted in Florida in 2006, in the Wakulla River. After that she started a journey to the unknown.

I was more determined than ever to pursue my career—it had taken on new meaning. I began to realize how little we really know about these animals and the way they move and cross deep ocean passages, like the Florida Straits—and how crucial it is that the United States and Cuba work together to learn about the marine life that ignores the political boundary that runs through the ninety nautical miles that separate the two countries. From that moment on, I started building a research project that would help me find answers to many of the existing questions about manatees. I had many dreams, and with them many challenges, as working with manatees in Cuba is not easy. For example, the car situation never changed.

As a biologist from the Center for Marine Research, University of Havana, I sought to fill an important gap existing in the knowledge of West Indian manatee: the Cuba population. By my side, teaching, inspiring, and supporting my work, were Dr. James "Buddy" Powell of Sea to Shore Alliance, a Florida NGO dedicated to the conservation of manatees. I was full of passion and more than determined to accomplish this goal. However, I kept encountering challenges that could have been a perfect excuse to give up. It was not only that I was trying to generate information on a small, elusive, inaccessible, and endangered population across over five thousand miles of coastline (more than Florida). More important, the resources needed to undertake this gargantuan task were really limited. These hurdles were not great for my career as a scientist expected to publish an article per year. Under this scenario, the scientific productivity was going to be as slow as the slowest manatee. But it didn't matter. While my brain was setting the path to take, my heart had the wheel. No rush. The PhD I intended to pursue had to wait a little bit.

A year later, I started a research project at Isla de la Juventud, in southern Cuba, a quietly magical place of mangrove forests and dark waters. There, I learned about manatee movements, habitat use, and behavior. I also learned from fishermen stories and their experiences. I learned about the eternal love between a manatee and a fisherman, a love that can kill (but only the manatee). Humans have been exploiting manatees since their arrival in the Caribbean thousands of years ago. First were the aborigines, then the colonizers, and today Cuba remains one of the few places in the range of this species where manatee meat is still used as a source of proteins. While learning about the natural history of these amazing creatures, I tried to show the fishers that there is also a world where manatees and fishermen can live happily ever after.

It was on that remote island that I captured and tagged for the first time a Cuban manatee to document its movement. The first capture for research purposes of a Florida manatee was in the 1970s. I was doing the same type of capture in 2012, more than fifty years later, after almost two years of dealing with paperwork and permit issues. But I did it. With a sense of accomplishment, to say nothing of euphoria, I successfully captured and tagged my first manatee. She was beautiful, and terrified, and my heart was racing faster than ever. Her skin was free of any scar, yet she was in great danger. I got to know the places she visited frequently, where she found freshwater, and what she ate. She took me to other manatees, and I learned why manatees were on that island. Isla de la Juventud (Isle of Youth), first known as Isle of Pine and Isle of Parrots, was not only a paradise for pines and parrots, manatees are able to find quiet and warm places to rest, and bottoms covered by rich and dense seagrass beds that they use as food.

Presumably seeking the same, Daysi and her calf, not yet a year old, had traveled to Cuba before President Barack Obama announced the re-opening of relations between the two countries. Ten years later, at the beginning of the Donald Trump era, another manatee traversed the Florida Straits to reach the warm waters of the Cuba Archipelago. In the more recent political environment, new impositions restricted any type of interaction between Cubans and Americans, but natural interactions persisted. The journey of these manatees demonstrated the ecological bridge between our nations, stronger than any political force or unnatural boundary. Political and economic tensions between Cuba and the United States began to build in 1959. But while the two governments stewed over politics, ecosystems and wildlife maintained their natural connections. Manatees are proof of that.

However, scientists to date know little about migration between Florida and Cuba beyond these single commutes. It is very hard to be sure why this body-scarred mother and her calf set off across the straits. Their travels raise a handful of questions waiting for answers. Are migrations common, and do they happen because manatees become lost in their search for warm water? Or is it that finding a suitable place to graze and stay during the winter has become more difficult as human population growth, development, freshwater depletion, and other pressures impact their habitat in Florida? It is difficult to say, and maybe both are the cause. Answers demand collaboration between the two countries in research, wildlife management, and conservation.

Manatees in Florida are described as a different subspecies from those in the West Indies and Cuba. After being isolated for a long time, it is believed that these two populations developed differences in the shape of their skulls. While found primarily in Florida, the Florida manatee occasionally ventures as far north as Virginia and, on rare occasions, Massachusetts. Along the Gulf of Mexico, Florida manatees can be found all the way over in Texas. Before the report of these long-distance travelers, a Florida migrant to Cuban waters was unknown. It was thought that individuals of this population could reach only the Bahamas and no farther south than the Dry Tortugas.

But manatees today may be moving between Cuba and Florida again, as they once may have done during past periods of population expansion and contraction. The Cuban and Florida manatees have different habitat requirements. A Florida manatee depends on warm-water refuges and the skill to evade boaters. A manatee in Cuba is influenced more by the accessibility of freshwater and the challenge to stay alive among poachers. Likewise, different histories of interactions with humans pose different challenges for their conservation in the two regions. Would Daysi and her calf, for example, know to avoid poachers?

A significant decline in the population between the late 1800s and passage of the Endangered Species Act in 1973 led to including the West Indian manatee as an endangered species in the United States. During the last forty years, their numbers in Florida have climbed from eight hundred individuals in the 1970s to at least six thousand today. Based on this successful population regrowth, the federal government downlisted the manatee to a threatened species.

The Cuban manatee population, by contrast, has been declining for many years. While they may not be sliced by boat propellers, manatees in Cuba, like other marine species, face many challenges, including a lack of enforcement of existing regulations and protection against human incursions. Poaching and inappropriate fishing gear are, at the moment, uncontrolled pressures that, in combination with the country's economic situation, kill untold numbers of manatees in Cuba. Insufficient scientific research there also means insufficient data on the population.

The recovery of the Florida manatee may be a model to reverse the plight of the Cuban manatee, especially since the region seems to be exchanging individuals.

The questions that emerged from these findings needed answers, and Florida was not only the right place for me to seek them, but also a wonderful place to learn about how strong and resilient manatees can be with a little help from humans. I was ready, then, for the next adventure of my life: the PhD journey. For a long time I'd been dreaming of continuing my studies in the home of the first manatee I saw. But going to Florida was not easy for a woman like me. Once again, diplomatic relations and political issues were taking its toll on science and conservation. For five years, I had been trying to get accepted at the University of Florida, until 2015, when the School of Natural Resources and Environment opened the doors and offered me an ideal environment for learning, doing science, and saving the manatees, my favorite things in the world.

I came to Florida with a brain full of ideas and a heart full of emotions. I felt welcome. I settled into a lovely and stimulating environment. I loved swimming in Daysi's first home, Three Sisters Springs at Crystal River, and I keep doing that. Florida's springs bring such a joy to my soul. It is like swimming inside a diamond of water where I can contemplate my favorite giants dancing, roaming peacefully, and resting easily. I feel a deep appreciation for these vulnerable ecosystems, as they have been a "warm" home for manatees in moments of coldness. In this case, the word "warm" is relative, as to me, a tropical woman, the 72-degree waters of the springs can be stinging; however, my heart warms up once I encounter a manatee. I suddenly cease to feel the cold. I'm thankful for Florida and its springs, as they allow me to be so close to manatees. In Cuba, swimming with a manatee is a rare treat, as they are very elusive. I don't blame them; that's how they must deal with the peril of hunters and nets.

In Florida, manatees are so friendly with and curious about people, and I think it was this special bond between Floridians and manatees that saved this population from disappearing. I know it is not enough, as habitat alteration and the greed for motorized speed are still snatching away the lives of many manatees. However, it is remarkable how Floridians love manatees, and my goal is to help instill that connection between nature and people in my country, and see Cubans feeling that same love for manatees that I have experienced and witnessed in Florida.

The PhD helped me answer some questions, and led to new ones. That's the wonder of science, the persistent pursuit of the truth. My love for nature, the sea, and the manatees has grown stronger, and I am determined to continue the next chapter of my life. Florida is now home and gave me both my son and a PhD, but Cuba is still in my blood and heart. Now, I feel the responsibility to contribute to preserving both Cuban and Florida ocean treasures and the natural bridge between them. To accomplish this, much needs to be done on both sides of the straits. A necessity, yet surely a challenge, is to achieve co-management of common habitat and natural resources, but for that to happen, Cuba and the United States must sit together at the table.

Cuba has a marine biodiversity considered unparalleled in the hemisphere; however, anthropogenic pressures are affecting local populations of marine species across the country. More than fifteen years of research and studies has shown me that manatees in Cuba might be suffering the consequences of years of exploitation. Interestingly, the research is also revealing the role of this population as an important hub leading to a regional connection of other manatee populations. But, for me, these results are not fully realized until they are translated into good conservation practices. Today, I am honored to continue doing science and conservation as part of the Clearwater Marine Aquarium's research department—an opportunity that will allow me to keep exploring the world of manatees, marine mammals, and the ocean. An opportunity I will use to keep inspiring people.

While politics has taken the lead role in U.S.–Cuban relations for half a century, it's now the ocean's turn. Separated by so few miles, Florida and Cuba can work together to safeguard their common bond and common interest in a sustainable sea, where manatees and many other marine creatures can swim freely, rather than dodge dangers on both sides. I believe this is the only way to eliminate the shadow of extinction that still hangs over many vulnerable manatee populations. After all, humans are the common element in this crisis. I never saw Daysi again in Cuba. She hasn't been seen in Florida, either. I keep searching for her, as I do for the answers to saving our shared sea.

Woodpeckers and Wildness

The Disney Wilderness Preserve

LESLIE K. POOLE

A spring breeze swirls under the vibrant blue ether as I inhale, pausing to switch the twenty-pound pole to my left shoulder. Sweat dribbles down my neck when I resume the trek through the thigh-high palmettos, trying to keep up with my energetic expedition leader, Beatriz Pace-Aldana.

"B" stops ahead under a tall pine tree girded with a white paint stripe. Upward, she points. And there it is: a small hole fifteen feet high, surrounded by thick bark and dripping with gooey sap. We quickly attach a small, slender "peeper-scope" to the end of the telescoping pole, adjusting and wiggling it until the camera slips into the gap. Looking at a handheld monitor, we exhale with excitement: three tiny fuzzballs are peering back, expecting a meal.

This is success—a trio of newborn red-cockaded woodpeckers, once commonplace throughout the southeastern United States but now listed as a federally endangered species. The birds are on the brink of extinction because of their need to nest in living longleaf pine trees that once blanketed Florida north of Lake Okeechobee and ranged through most of the southeastern United States. But with human development, logging, and turpentine operations in the nineteenth century, some 98 percent of longleaf disappeared, one of the worst habitat losses in the world. That we are observing them through a wobbling camera rig in a place that was once a logged-over cattle ranch, and later planned to become a housing development, is a minor miracle and proof that some "wildness" can be restored to Florida—a dream and promise for future generations.

That vision is being realized at the Disney Wilderness Preserve (DWP), an 11,500-acre tract located at the edge of Central Florida's suburban chaos. The preserve's name is a paradox—Disney and the resulting theme park boom are the engines that turned the rural citrus-growing region into a traffic and development nightmare, displacing wildlife, wetlands, and forests. But the preserve, run by The Nature Conservancy (TNC) since 1992, also exists thanks to Disney, which led the way in the development and funding for it in order to mitigate wetland destruction and impacts caused by construction of its Animal Kingdom theme park and the nearby Celebration community. Other groups, including the Orlando Aviation Authority, also added acres and funds. As a result, DWP is the first large-scale off-site restoration project of its kind, setting an example of how collaboration between diverse partners can create something "wild" in a place where nature is slowly vanishing.

Ah, the irony. But ahhhh, the wonderful result.

A view across the preserve of green, gold, and brown—at sedges, Lopsided Indian grass, and palmettos—resembles what native people and early pioneers may have encountered. The tall stands of longleaf are thriving once again, their needles singing an aeolian harmony as the wind rises. That, to me, is the specialness of this space: that it looks natural, untouched by modern technology. Which can't be further from the truth.

For two decades after its creation, DWP managers and scientists studied, planned, and then carried out a careful strategy for ecosystem management to bring it back to "nature." They removed non-native species, filled in twenty miles of ten-foot-deep ditches, and removed dikes to restore natural water flow. Importantly, they brought fire back to the landscape through regular controlled burns that simulate historic burns. As a result, the preserve's flatwoods, scrub habitat, and four thousand acres of wetlands have returned to a semblance of normal, especially important since the preserve is part of the headwaters of the beleaguered Everglades drainage system, now the focus of an $8 billion federal-state restoration effort.

I first visited DWP with my family in the early 1990s. I had met some TNC folks whose excitement about the project was palpable. They invited me to stay in a cabin—really an old two-bedroom trailer that had been used by previous owners as a hunting camp. I immediately said yes, borrowed a friend's SUV to negotiate the dirt roads, and brought along my husband and two young sons for a weekend adventure.

As far as I know, we were the only people on the property that autumn weekend, but we were rarely alone as magic swirled about us.

A pair of fearless sandhill cranes greeted us as we unloaded the car. We were entranced by their grace, while a bit fearful of their long, eye-level beaks. At sunrise, a flock of turkey hens circled the cabin, while a male "tom" spread his tail feathers and chased them with ardent calls of love. My sons were briefly impressed before demanding breakfast. I was mesmerized.

Later that day, we carefully drove down dirt roads, scaring up more turkeys. And the boys were tickled to find animal bones, a snake dozing in the sun, and an armadillo on an afternoon hike. They felt like real explorers, especially when we realized that the oak hammock shading our cabin was likely the site of a native hunting camp hundreds of years ago. No telephones, no television, and no one cared.

Through the years I've visited DWP to witness its slow evolution. The ditches are long gone, although vague scars remain where they once existed. Regular burning has reduced overgrown stands of plants and invasive species, clearing out the understory like a vacuum so that natural grasses can flourish.

I've done my best to share this treasure, hiking sandy paths with friends and taking my college classes there on field trips. While I was overjoyed during one trip to see an endangered Florida scrub-jay—a bird found only in the state's scrub habitat—my students were more excited by a deer crossing the road. The scrub-jay has highly specific needs, including an ecosystem that regularly burns, another indicator of the DWP's vitality. As much as I tried to convey that the scrub-jay was really "cool," I think the class preferred Bambi, as well as their ride on an oversized swamp buggy through the backwoods.

Last year, my husband and I joined friends to canoe on Lake Russell, along the preserve's eastern border. Little development has occurred on its tannin-colored waters, and we were awed to find a large colony of wading birds, including bright pink roseate spoonbills, taking advantage of the tranquility. Other times I've marveled at the brief but bounteous spring bloom of wild purple irises in lakeshore wetlands. And when students dip their hands into the lake, I remind them that they are touching Everglades waters—that the drips from their fingers meander all the way to the southern tip of the state without ever again being this pristine.

And that's the truth about Florida—indeed of the world—today. Few unspoiled spots of nature exist. To believe there are areas of true wilderness, defined by the federal 1964 Wilderness Act as "an area where the earth and its community of life are untrammeled by man," is preposterous. Our pollution has reached the highest points of the atmosphere and the deepest depths of the oceans. We left old equipment on the moon and regularly export technology, destined to eventually cease working, into our solar system and beyond.

In this way, the Disney Wilderness Preserve, despite its name, is in no respect a true wilderness. This is abundantly clear to most visitors, who, if they traveled the same route as I did on a recent weekday, had to endure a seventy-five-minute, thirty-seven-mile slog on a construction-congested Interstate 4 and a winding path through the rapidly developing suburbia of Poinciana in western Osceola County. Across from the DWP gate lie a church and school and advancing subdivisions, as the preserve becomes increasingly hemmed in by development.

And yet, once inside its gates, the sense of peace and beauty is overwhelming. And there is that smell—of pine, grass, water—of wild Florida that is becoming increasingly hard to find. My blood pressure surely drops twenty points; the knots in my neck relax.

So, if it isn't a wilderness, what is DWP?

I posed this question to TNC's Zach Prusak, charged with bringing attention to the site. He calls it "wilderness now" and notes that for the preserve's nine thousand annual visitors, many from different states and countries, "this is some of the first and only wilderness they will see." It may be their first glimpse of old Florida, of healthy ecosystems that once spanned the state. So, it is valuable, useful nature but with a new definition and goal.

"In Wildness is the preservation of the world," wrote Henry David Thoreau in 1862. The American Transcendentalist writer believed that one could best find spirituality in nature. He lamented that people of his era were losing touch with the wild and predicted that such a void ultimately would hurt their souls and civilization. This is the man who viewed a swamp as a sacred place—a *sanctum sanctorum*. His was a far cry from the calls of manifest destiny in the nineteenth century that drove settlers to conquer North America from sea to shining sea, plowing up prairies and tearing down forests along the way. But Thoreau's words resonate deeply today, connecting his era to ours, his echoes spurring work to save and restore Florida's wild places.

They are there in the faces of the husband and wife sitting quietly at a bench overlooking a pond where a wading bird stalks through the grass. They are in the cry of a red-shouldered hawk that alights on a fence pole at sunset, the evening glow shimmering through its feathers. You hear them in the laughter of children running on the grass near a visitor center, stopping to look at a butterfly on a bloom. Here is beauty. Here is grace. But one must stop, like Thoreau, and find it.

Zach Prusak envisions DWP becoming a collaborative center for ecological science. There are talks of creating dormitories to house visiting scientists and scholars in different fields for extended periods of time. Already groups from the University of Central Florida and the National Ecological Observatory Network are conducting research on a variety of issues, including climate change. There may be opportunities to certify students in conducting controlled burns as well, an especially important component in Florida ecological restoration and management. It is, in Zach's words, "repurposing wilderness."

The preserve also serves a larger function in the maintenance of statewide ecology. It is part of a system of large tracts of land that managers and planners are trying to connect so that large animals can travel through the state. These wildlife corridors include national and state parks and forests, preserves, and privately held lands, including many large cattle ranches. They will be essential in the future to allow Florida black bears and Florida panthers—the latter highly endangered—to move in search of food, territory, and love. Connecting with other animals across the peninsula may spur healthier populations and increased genetic diversity, important to the survival and resiliency of these beloved mammals.

Florida panthers, which once roamed the South, have for decades been forced into the Everglades and Big Cypress Swamp. Disappearing habitat combined with a loss of genetic diversity dropped their numbers to an alarming twenty to thirty by 1995. But protective laws and an unprecedented program that brought Texas panthers into the state to breed with native cats and improve the mammals' genetics has paid off with an estimated 120 to 230 adults today. That means young Florida panthers must expand northward into new territory—one was tracked wandering through DWP in recent years, a reason for celebration.

The return of the red-cockaded woodpecker is another point of pride.

The tiny seven-inch black-and-white birds (red-cockaded refers to a barely discernable spot on the side of the males' heads) were extirpated from the area since the 1960s, the result of extensive logging of longleaf pines. The birds, with an estimated total population of ten thousand, which was on decline as they became increasingly isolated, were declared a federally endangered species in 1970, triggering actions to improve their numbers. One method was to find places to reintroduce them.

In 2007, the U.S. Fish & Wildlife Service, working with DWP, brought a group of juvenile birds into the preserve's restored longleaf habitat. The birds came from healthy southeastern populations, including those at Florida's Apalachicola National Forest, Osceola National Forest, Withlacoochee State Forest, and Fort Stewart in South Carolina.

At DWP, the birds were carefully placed into wooden boxes—one male and one female in each—built by land managers to mimic woodpecker cavities. The artificial nests, with round holes for egress, were located ten to twenty feet high inside clusters of healthy longleaf pines to house the new residents, replicating the communities of four to five cavities that the birds usually create for themselves. Then scientists waited and watched.

Many things can go wrong with nesting—the translocated pairs may not produce eggs, the eggs may not be viable, and, despite the sticky sap, snakes and other birds may get into nests and eat eggs or kill babies. Each nest has two to four eggs that hatch after eleven days, leaving very vulnerable offspring. Parents immediately start searching for insects to feed the babies, which, if all goes well, will have feathers at sixteen days and be ready to fly ten days later.

By 2010, DWP scientists were celebrating the survival of four fledglings. Today, a third of the birds on the property are "natural"—not brought in from other places. The woodpeckers increasingly are creating their own cavities—ten currently—reducing their use of human-made ones. Nature is becoming natural.

My mid-May expedition with "B" came at the beginning of hatching season, her sixth spent monitoring the woodpeckers. The birds started nesting in mid-April, and on today's trek we have checked twelve clusters, finding four confirmed nests with a total of three eggs and eight chicks. One nest couldn't be scoped because of an adult woodpecker who wouldn't leave (a sign babies were probably inside); another revealed an encroaching red-bellied woodpecker looking back at us. A very good day overall. The numbers are low, but the population is growing, and that is the ultimate goal.

In coming weeks, "B" will monitor the nests and tag babies to keep records of the population. So far, the federal efforts are paying off, as the woodpeckers are now estimated at more than fourteen thousand living in eleven states. But it's not just the woodpeckers that benefit from this program: at least twenty-seven species of animals rely on the cavities for roosting or nesting, including other birds, squirrels, frogs, and lizards. Everything is connected.

As "B" and I pause to eat our bag lunches, leaning against the pickup truck, I look up. High overhead, the sun is surrounded by a circular rainbow, known as a solar halo. I'm told it is a rare sign. Today, I take it as a good omen for the fate of these tiny birds and of the future hopes for restoring and protecting Florida's wild landscapes.

Sighting by the St. Johns

RUSS KESLER

It took four lanes
in three low surges,
brown under the pink tongue of morning,
then was gone
in a hole it opened
in the roadside weeds.

Panther, moving north
with the coiling river
into miles of grass,
leaving a print slowly filling
with dark water.

If I'd been looking
in the rearview
I'd have missed it, perhaps
noticed the sedge quivering
and driven on.

But I was watching
the river mist over the road,
ready for the shadow
that rose and disappeared,
lean ghost with light at its heels.

PART IV

WATER

Up the Okalawaha

A Sail into Fairy-Land

HARRIET BEECHER STOWE

(*CHRISTIAN UNION*, MAY 14, 1873)

We have done it! Whether in the body or out, we have been to dream-land, to the land of the fays and the elves, the land where reality ceases and romance begins. In the measurement of earth and in the geographic language of reality this was accomplished in a six days' journey, on the little steamer Okalawaha. We left Mandarin at eleven o'clock on Thursday, March 27, and returned to it again the next Tuesday afternoon. We had often noticed, passing by on the river, the little steamer Okalawaha, looking for all the world like a gray square cotton bale, and we confess that we shuddered at the idea of going on a bush-whacking tour through the native swamps of the alligator in such a suspicious looking craft as that.

But the experiences of more venturesome friends, who dared and did— went up and came back with songs of joy upon their heads—persuaded us. Our tourist friends, persons of renowned good sense, came back from their trip fairly inebriated with enthusiasm, wild with incoherent raptures. They had seen Europe and Italy, Naples and the blue grotto, but never, never had they in their lives seen aught so entrancing as this. It was a spectacle, weird, wondrous, magical—to be remembered as one of the things of a lifetime.

Well, really, after this who would not expect to be disappointed? Who, going with such a fanfaronade of expectations, would not come on back a little worse for experience? Nevertheless we have been, and come back, and are not disappointed, but prepared to chorus the most extravagant laudations of our friends. How it is we know not. You know it is a wide-attested fact that there are places and regions on earth where the fays and the dryads and other wood spirits still live, who enchant the eyes of the comer and bear him off into magical regions, and bewilder him till he don't know whether he has been on earth or under it. We have almost forgotten our classical literature, but we dimly remember the Cave of Trophonius and the shades of the Delphic Oracle, and Lake Avernus, whence Virgil descended into the Elysian Fields. The fountain of immortal youth, which Ponce de Leon supposed was to be found in the heart of Florida, could have been no other than the Silver Spring, whose magical waters, like a great glancing chrysolite, lie in the heart of these unknown forests.

So, while you, my poor, dear, virtuous friends were fighting with roaring March winds up in the "still vexed" North, behold us stepping on board the little steamer Okalawaha on a bright day, with a gay and festive party of young people. To begin with, our boat was an agreeable disappointment. We had always dreaded the boat as the abatement of the pleasure; for what, we said, could be done with twenty passengers on such a little craft? We found, however, a neat, well-ventilated cabin, with berths for eight ladies, as comfortable as could be desired. Then there were six more state-rooms, opening from the central cabin, of two berths each. The captain was all accommodation; every hand on board, cook, steward, waiter were as good natured and obliging as could be desired, and the passengers, in return, were good natured; polite to each other, and unexacting in their requirements; and so the little bark came to be looked on as quite a nice little home. As to our table, it was crowded, to be sure, both with dishes and with guests; and as the whole cookery had to be done in a place no bigger than a good-sized pocket handkerchief, the results were certainly not to be severely criticized. If the proof of the pudding be in the eating, certainly the guests did ample justice to their meals, eating to right and left in a most complimentary manner. In fact, although we started on this expedition feeling rather poorly, and with a very faint appetite, we became uncritical devourers of whatever was set before us, merely from living all day in the fine open air that blew across the boat's deck.

Our voyage circumstantially may be thus narrated:

From the pier in Mandarin, as aforementioned, we stepped aboard, about eleven o'clock in the forenoon of Thursday. Our little slow stern-wheel boat made the best of her way upward and reached Palatka just about seven o'clock. The boat lay there an hour or two, then we all took to our berths, opened our little slides of windows for the river breeze to blow through, and resigned ourselves peacefully to sleep. In the middle of the night we were waked by the scraping of branches against our little boat, and looked dreamily out to see that we were gliding through palmetto forests and weird grottos, lit up with blazing pine torches. It seemed part of a fantastic dream as our weary eyes closed and the boat rippled on.

Friday morning we were waked by the singing of birds in the branches, to find ourselves still gliding through the arches of an unbroken forest. We sat on a little platform in front of the pilot-house, and glided along, seeing into the very heart of the tropical mysteries.

Sometimes the whole way seemed given up to palmetto groves—rising in every conceivable shape and variety—growing with a luxuriance and a grace indescribable. The trunk of the palms sometimes seems a regular and exact pillar of basket-work, built up twenty or thirty feet. In the crevices of the basket-work large ferns and air plants take root, so that the tree is often a pillar of various foliage and flowers.

Here and there the palms lean aslant over the water; they throw themselves forward and meet in arches overhead; they lie creeping in scaly folds on the ground; they wave sixty or seventy feet high in the air. The oldest palms have shed the scaly basket-like enclosure, and are round and smooth like columns, the latest scales only remaining high up in the air, and the ferns and vines waving from them like streamers. But by far the greater part of the way, the palmetto was gracefully intermixed with other trees. The cypress, with its glistening white trunk and shapely pillars, rises to an immense height; its snowy columns reflected far down in the smooth glassy water. The palms sometimes seemed embraced in the white arms of cypress, leaning their plumy heads against its branches, their dusky hue contrasting with the vivid yellow green of the cypress feathers. The other trees were the water-ash, the loblolly bay, the magnolia glauca, certain varieties of red maple and water-oaks, and a few of the magnolia grandiflora. Growth seemed to have run riot here, to have broken into strange goblin forms, such as Doré might have chosen for his weird imagining. Here, where foraged nature has been let alone, where the fiery heats and the moist soil have conspired together, there is a netting and convoluting, a twisting and weaving and intertwining of all sorts of growths; and one might fancy it an enchanted forest, where the trees were going to change into something new and unheard of.

The alligator seems to belong most naturally in these shades. The long-necked water-turkey sits perched gravely on the boughs overhead, or dives in the waters below. The limpkin, with its long neck and legs and its wild plaintive cry, the white crane and blue crane, the pink and white curlew, these seem the fit inhabitants for whom these forest solitudes are made. The dreamy wildness, the perfect strangeness of all this, its utter unlikeness to anything one has ever seen, inclines one to aimless reverie. The stories of Tick and Touquet seem quite possible here.

The boat glides on, from hour to hour, as the river winds and turns, and doubles upon itself, with still the same flowery solitudes reverberating with the same wild cries of birds, glittering with slanting sunbeams, festooned with waving garlands that hang from tree to tree.

At intervals the steam-whistle startles the birds and makes the forest echoes ring—it is a sign that we are coming to a landing.

The inhabited country of this region is an elevated tract that lies back of the river, and these landings are breathing holes, vistas opening from the interminable forest mystery into human abodes. Generally, at one of these landings a letter-box is nailed up conspicuously on the trunk of some cypress or other large tree, where letters and papers are left for the families whose invisible homes lie beyond.

Sometimes a group of two or three smart hunters in high-peaked hats, attired in homespun garments with knives in their boots, stood leaning on their guns, waiting the approach of the boat. They seemed a grave, taciturn, unsmiling race, long-haired, bearded, and roughly attired, with the shallow complexion and dark eyes that gave intimations of Minorcan blood.* They reminded us of the shepherds of the Campania. Occasionally a wild turkey or a saddle of venison, hung in the tree, promised a supply to the provision market of the boat. They brought pailfuls of new-laid eggs and sometimes baskets of great golden oranges, which the captain bought and dispensed liberally among the passengers. The weekly touching of the boats at these lonely landings are the only communication these settlers hold with the outside world. A more solitary life cannot be imagined.

Perhaps our voyage through these unbroken forests might have been, in time, somewhat monotonous, had not a dozen or two mighty hunters kept us from going to sleep by the briskness of their firing. There were on board a few good marksmen, who knew how to hit what they fired at, but about an equal number of inexperienced hands, foaming at the mouth with excitement, and

---

* A Minorcan was a native of Menorca, one of the Balearic Islands of the Mediterranean Sea. The first came to Florida in the eighteenth century as indentured servants.

quite likely to hit any one of us as the alligators. The cry, "Dar's a 'gater," was a signal for a perfect fusillade, much more dangerous to us than to the alligators, who generally dove and paddled off.

The first day on board was a hot one, and was like a Fourth of July in a city, an unintermitted blaze and fizz. Every lady on board had a headache, and the coming on of night was a welcome relief. Then came the lighting of the great pine knot brazier over the pilot-house, and we sat on deck watching the weird effects of the fire light up the long watery aisles and colonnades of the palmy woods. Saturday morning we woke in the broad Savannahs. Waving fields of water plants, water lilies, yellow and white arrowheads, pickerel weed, water lettuce, and every other aquatic plant that can be thought of, were here in wide sweeping fields of undulating waves. It was a lake of lilies: tall bulrushes, six or seven feet high, waved and nodded, and on every bulrush perched a red-wing blackbird. It was a prairie of birds—they rose in clouds. They sang and capered, lit on the tip end of bulrushes, and slid down to the middle, then swung busily with their short airy whistle, the picture of joy. A beautiful little water bird, with blue feathers and red head and feet, flitted over the water-lily leaves, and one or two flocks of green and gold paroquets rose on wing and soared away.

The water-turkey and the blue and white crane, by their heedless conduct in perching squarely in sight of the boat, destroyed a great deal of our pleasure. We did not want to see them fall, mangled and fluttering, under the awkward shots of some of our sportsmen, and left to starve to death lingeringly, as the boat glided on.

The destructive instincts of the hunter seem to destroy all sympathy with nature, all sense of beauty of scenery, or interest in its various sources of knowledge.

The Savannahs, in which we sailed all day Saturday, gradually merge into a chain of beautiful lakes—Lakes Griffin, Eustace, and Harris. We entered Lake Griffin on Saturday evening. It is a charming sheet of water, with high banks, on some of which are fine building sites. In the dim gray of the dawn, Sunday morning, we woke to find ourselves tied up to a wharf at Okahumke. We turned over and went to sleep, and when we woke again the boat was far on her homeward way again. We were just passing out of Lake Eustace into Lake Griffin as we left the breakfast table. It was as lovely a day as heart could imagine, angelically clear and fresh, and our quartette sat on the deck and sang hymns in infinite variety.

In our youth a religious hymn was the most long-drawn and doleful sound conceivable. Now, under the genial culture of the Sunday-school, hymns have budded and blossomed; they are full of life, and color and motion.

Sunday night, the wonders of our voyage came to a climax. The captain had announced to us that the boat would enter the Silver Spring between one and two o'clock, and advised us to sit up if we wanted to see the very finest part of the route.

We did sit up, prepared as we were by a night's experience in wild forest traveling. We were taken by surprise by the wonderful scenes through which we passed.

We seemed floating through an immense cathedral whose white marble columns met in vast arches overhead and were reflected in the glassy depths below. The dusky plumes of the palmetto waving above, lit by torch-light, looked like the fine tracery of a wondrous sculptured roof. The brilliant under-white of the bay leaves, the transparent red of the water maple, and the soft vivid feathers of the cypress, had a magical brilliancy as our light passed through the wooded aisles. The reflected fire-light gave the most peculiar effect. Every trunk, and limb, and branch of the trees, down to the minutest spray, was of glistening whiteness, like ivory. The gray moss that streamed down seemed like crapy veils of silver, and was of a wonderful profusion, in some cases veiling the trees entirely.

In the stillness of the night our gliding boat seemed to float like a specter; clouds of fragrance were wafted to us from distant orange groves. The cranes and herons and wild wood birds would wake, dazed with the glare of our torches, and flutter into our very hands as we passed.

We took the one step from the sentimental to the ludicrous, when one of our party most unexpectedly captured a water-turkey from a bough just over our head, and held him aloft in wild excitement. The poor bird made the best use of his long, snaky neck, throwing himself, with open mouth, hither and thither among the company, with a plucky show of fight, till, between laughing and alarm, we were thoroughly discomposed and prevailed on his captor to throw him back into the trees.

What a night was that! Everybody watched and wondered, and the most prosaic grew poetic. About one o'clock we glided into the Silver Spring run, and by two, we were all gathered on the lower deck, looking down into transparent depths that gave the impression that our boat was moving through air. Every pebble and aquatic plant we glided over seemed, in the torch-light, invested with prismatic brightness. When the boat at last came to landing in the Silver Spring, we laid us down to sleep, fairly tired out with excitement, to wait for the morning.

Monday morning broke bright and beautiful, and there we lay in a little wooded basin a quarter of a mile in diameter, with all the underworld clearly revealed from its translucent depths. The water had the crystalline clearness and the magical prismatic reflections which give such charm to the blue grotto at Capri. Ribs of limestone rock are seen far down, and the spring boils and bubbles upward, throwing up thousands of gallons a minute without making more than a ripple on the surface.

A party of us got into a little skiff and floated over the transparent depth. Every variety of water plant was growing and waving over the varied surfaces of the bottom, which had its heights and depths, its caverns and grottos. We could see the fish darting hither and thither, and mark on the brilliant sands at the bottom various objects which had been thrown in by experimenting travelers. The water was of about the same high temperature with the spring at Green Cave. The shores were clothed with tropical forests all around, and here and there we could see starry flocks of a peculiar and beautiful white lily which grows abundantly on these waters. From a star-shaped calyx of six narrow white leaves comes out a silver cup; from the edges of this cup rise six stamens with their golden heads. . . .

As the boat passed from the shadows of the Okalawaha to the broad St. John's, three cheers made the woods ring, and our "camping in the wilderness" was over.

Musings

MARGARET ROSS TOLBERT

SPRINGS at NIGHT

We are on the Santa Fe River at Rum Island. Nearby, Todd
Taylor has set up elaborate structures with batteries and
lights, in kayaks, fishtanks, with tree-trimming tools, on
intricate floating PVC rigs, on and in the waters of the
Santa Fe and Rum Island springs.
Drawing in the dark
I am audience to tree branches stretched in the light,
leaning over a glassy black sea.
Springs at night—like seeing the other side of the moon
The face of the river
When the mask of sun, waves and visitors comes off
At the end of the day, the river shows another self.
A lamplighter in a small boat
Floating lanterns and homemade constructions.
Batteries in kayaks
Lights in fishtanks
Things shine with blooming, frozen intricacy.
Clumps (of what?) speed past in the current,
In continuous passage down a black river,
lanced with white trunks that gleam in the light

An endless stream that stops for no one.
We are either observers or part of the flow.
A mist shoulders in, a pale void that the trees approach
It blurs the outlines, the branches reach to touch it.
A mullet jumps, silver into the light.
Slowly the mist shifts downriver.
Water surface of brushed lacquer, black and glossy like a
grooved record. I want to dive through that shiny elastic
flow.
Cricket songs like soft tambourines.
Muffled explosions as nuts fall into the water. A chill
breeze blurs the outlines of reflections.
The river looks like a large square pond floating in space.
Giant eyes of shadow roar in the reflections.
Things fly by, pale objects stuck in the poured ink flow.
I get used to the intricacy and dazzle
Trees like a lace crinoline of light, each leaf crisply edged
with pearl.
The river is really the color of ink.
Tree trunks reflect in it as a condensation of pulsing lines,
lightly wrapped.
Surrounded by blackness,
nothing exists except the mirrored surface and the lighted
trees.

SALT SPRINGS

Instantly plug into the different energy of Salt Springs.
Water with a tang, like an acrid sports drink.
Yellow light snaps crackles up through the water like
flames.
From the walkway, a strange vista spread out below:
quadrilles of stone in mint green water, a kind of bobbing
baklava, Nazca lines made by the ancient hand of water.
Liquifying stair steps arc into the white ellipses of the boil
From below, looking up through the water, the sky a
warped blue shaped by stone pylons

Spring boils signposted by glassy surfaces
amidst choppy marks of the waves in the headspring.
Underwater, giant molars like flower buds begin to bloom
open in waves of light
Everything that thinks it is straight transformed into
arabesque motion and energy.
Become like the whimsical and wayward schools of fish,
tossed from one spring to the next.
A skate pressed into a crevice;
baleful glare
Blue crab flies like a bullet across the void
To others stuck, like butterflies, on the angles of the rock.
A blue crab like the Andromeda Galaxy angles down into
the eye's deep and violent abyss.
Another more intrepid crab crests a rock,
bold mien
I'm chased by a blue crab as I exit the depths.
Enter a vase shaped out of stone
A deep and narrow crucible for light
That streams like steam to the surface water
My head is upside down
wreathed in two currents of warm and cool water, chill
water and warmer.
I am in the vast columnar folds of a giant's molars. In a
brisk gale of stars and flecks.
I'm hanging on to edges of the great teeth.
Stay upside down.
Face into the current.
Like any fish.
An aquifer world streams past me.
Red orange flecks from the flow propel upward.
I can feel eyes upon me.
An armored catfish on the wall, drops like a weight, waves
down into the gloom of a cave opening
Colors crackle in an electric cloud of light. Fish winnow
the current in a shifting grid, flash in the distance, rub
down in the creases and valleys of rock.
Toward the river the floor rises, spreads out a carpet of

snails, long gone

No one in the shells.

Rush out, time to paint at the edge of the springs.

"Cartouches of enamel clear water encircled by waves, escutcheons of calm."

Oh, I want these descriptions to represent the norm in the world.

Lost in contemplation.

(And then:

A man stumbles up the walk toward me as I paint. Just steps away he clambers up into a bush and defecates violently. I retreat to a safe distance.

It's a long wait.

"I'm waiting for you to finish," I finally say.

"I had a little emergency," he says.

He finally finishes, leaving behind banners of toilet paper still caught on the bushes.)

A TREE in a SPRING

If a tree falls in the springs, did it mean to?
At Bozell Springs on the Chipola River, a tree in a spring.
It is a narrow spring, one of four in sequence.
Each spring with a miniature turquoise fairyland beneath:
crags and precipices, castle towers and deep valleys,
rocky stone bridges picked out in a beam of sunlight. The
beam passes slowly, picking out minute details and
structures.
Like a twist of a kaleidoscope and then
Each tiny part is illuminated.
It was late spring.
Trees seem to love to touch the water,
But they hesitate at water's edge.
Well not this one.
This tree had to go in.
I don't remember if the leaves were gold.
Or crystal?

It's confusing because
They were all lighted up.
I don't remember roots.
So here's how it went down:
The tree cast itself in the water,
like a lance.
It dove in.
And it became light.
Light glowing everywhere as we swam in and around the
branches. At once gilded with light, and flashing it.
(I had my camera. It took part in every arabesque, every
intricate move I made as I climbed down the tree into the
springs.
And then, in the next spring the next day, the camera fell
into the 10-ft eelgrass, an optical illusion of waving forms
in flecks of light, and it's probably still there.)
What does the spring do?
From the rocky labyrinth far below,
the sand flies high in the spring, a skyward arc
then it settles back, sliding down
the leaves of the tree.
If you dusted for fingerprints
you could not dust any more thoroughly
than the fingers of the aquifer
sifting sand over each surface
Aquifer snow falling
In an upside-down world.

FERN HAMMOCK and JUNIPER SPRINGS

Off in the Ocala National Forest, springs flow into Juniper
Run that wends its way down to Lake George. The
headspring forms a deep pool with a mill wheel. Nearby
Fern Hammock springs are lava lamp orbs of turquoise
floating in a pool, where water puffs out of sand boils.
*No headspring visit today; mother bear and cubs wander
in Juniper.*

Walk slowly at Fern Hammock towards the bridge, wild
turkeys ahead.
Not a passive landscape, there for the taking;
This is a restive subject,
ever changing.
Sand boils like smoke rings.
A live oak leans over and touches a blue boil, rimmed with
bistre from infinite rings of silt.
One blue eye, porthole to the aquifer,
crossed by a phalanx of fish
sand boils
flying at me
they seem to generate their own phosphoresce
Blooms of light in a gloom of forest shade
Gurgling water to a surface of taffy colored sand
A vine like a bad signature moves back and forth across it
A cloud of gnats occupies a spot of night
Fish coalesce and fan out across a luminous plain of light.
A submerged palm trunk is a dark figurehead against a
bright sea.
Cabbage palm's shadow like liberty's crown,
Rarefied Martian atmosphere where far away mountains
seem close.
Ripples like hand claps
leapfrog across the stillness
Minute fish flee from a sudden furious belching of water,
and then return to swim boldly across a minute Charybdis
in reverse.
A branch
takes a diagonal to the water
A scallop of tightly wound wood
Scattered opals fester aloft in nothingness.
SILVER GLEN SPRINGS
At Silver Glen,
A sleeping manatee
like a carving out of blue stone.
every ten minutes it rose to touch the surface to breathe
Then sank back down.

SILVER SPRINGS

Urban spring, big as a city,
A reputation: the world's most famous spring.
Suburbs, next to the magical springs
People push a stroller with a crying baby.
Silver Springs exudes a kind of gargantuan languor. Or
maybe it just gave up.
Now the clumps of eelgrass fuse with a muddy thatch of
algae, like flattened giant air plants on the river bottom.
Blue fish flash by.
But then later, in deep valleys
eelgrass like a forest of knitting needles, stroked clean of
algae by the current.
It's fish.
Friendly fish.
Fish of all kinds circle the boat.
Giant largemouth bass.
A gar rising toward me like a floating log.
A bowfin like a barrel checks me out, dorsal fin rippling
continuously.
In high-water desperation,
turtles on a submerged log piled up like cars in a
junkyard.
It's color.
Fingers of turquoise reach along the river bottom.
Ripples rush over the voice of the aquifer far below.
Springs far below, kayakers and boaters above.
Too deep, too distant to really experience.
In this deep spring, a disconnect, a delay
Open-mouthed springs vent, in silence far below
A ventriloquism of force in a slick of water on the surface
above.
Shaggy crowns of submerged palms emerge from the
water.
Imposing fake forts and monumental alligators on the
banks.
A capsized shed, turtles' toenails scratch on the tin roof

as they clamber into the sunlight.
Boils in the river
Framed by eelgrass, curled and crimped in the water's
distortion
Float out in a blue void.
What is the color of the spring? It's *turquoise*
Next to reflections of white clouds in a sky of *cobalt blue*
Same value
And yet in the midst of this urban spring, here is true
nature.
Giant alligators on display,
unmoved by our presence
wildlife accustomed to humans.
We are no threat.
We are no big deal.
We are like any other fish or bird, finding our place down
the hierarchy of the water world.

BLUE SPRINGS—2018

Gilchrist Blue Springs has changed and I want the old
one back
Stepping in the water, the moire instantly swings into
action.
It radiates out
My own aura.
I swim up to a young man, who, neck down, is enveloped
in a cloud of blue, turquoise, and purple. It shifts and
radiates. Does he know this?
It looks like the world of land and water and all possible
hues spread out around him. Do I look like this when
someone sees me in the water?
Missing the underwater gardens of Gilchrist Blue Springs
Down the springs run.
We pass the occasional turtle and trundle down the run.
It is desolate and clean of plant life
A cold blue horizon of poured silver arcs over my head.

The only clear route for me to travel is into the reflection.
There are inroads of algae dripping off roots
Dollar weed is in hand-to-hand combat, re-colonizing the
white sand bottom of the springs run.
I bottom out on the run and look up.
Like clearing a spot on a misted window
I can have a vantage point looking through the silver
ceiling of the run.
I can look up through an apron of reflections and see
trees like spires high overhead.
Like Alice's mirror, when I look directly at the silvered
surface it melts away and shows the schema of another
world on the other side of the looking glass.
As I reach the vents of Naked Springs a conflagration of
Ludwigia, like brilliant lettuce-colored drops, shoots out on
a line into the current.

The Pulse of Paynes Prairie

LARS ANDERSEN

Something is sloshing. I hear it only vaguely at the edge of my awareness as I scan my surroundings.

Panning the view from left to right, I make a mental accounting of features I've known my whole life but, today, are somehow different. There's the small, hyacinth-covered cove of Alachua Sink, nestled into the base of a steep, tree-shrouded bluff to my left.

The sloshes are coming in sets now, like waves onto a beach. They grow louder, peak, and then fade away. Slosh, sloSH, SLOSH, SLosh, slosh.

In the eleven o'clock direction from where I'm facing, a large bay occupies an area that is usually a well-defined lake—the large, eastern lobe of Alachua Sink—where visitors often come to view alligators sunning on the sloped, sandy shore.

slosh, sloSH, SLOSH, SLosh, slosh.

To my right, Paynes Prairie is not the marshy savanna of the past half century, but a vast lake, thickly adorned with floating plants and emergent vegetation. It is nearly ten feet deep in the center.

slosh, sloSH, SLOSH, SLOsh, slosh.

It's like that with epiphanies. One minute I'm slogging in knee-deep water that is usually a dry hiking trail, the next, something I see or hear—maybe the rhythmic sloshing of feet that sounds vaguely like a beating heart—sparks an idea that morphs into an exciting insight about the terrain. I pause to contemplate and am lost in those thoughts when suddenly something grabs my attention and reminds me that I am supposed to be leading a tour. One hundred yards ahead are the twenty customers who had been slogging down the trail behind me with their kayaks in tow. They now are in deeper water, climbing into their boats.

The epiphany that struck me this morning on La Chua Trail lingered in my mind the rest of the day. Every so often, my thoughts returned to the questions spawned by the sound of those slogging feet. Given that this is the third basin-filling flood in twenty years and that such flooding hadn't happened for over half a century before, is it possible that Paynes Prairie's water cycle is slowly returning to normal? After massive efforts to divert and drain away the prairie's life-blood of water, are the recent efforts to restore it actually working?"

. . .

As natural features go, Paynes Prairie is one of the most unique in Florida. Its basic design—a twenty-square-mile basin with a water-tight bottom—is that of a lake. Yet, it never fills. All water that enters the basin floor as rain or in small streams drains away through a crack in the limestone floor of Alachua Sink, a large sinkhole on the prairie's north edge. This vent, while probably smaller than a canoe (a comparison my tour groups find comforting), is the only thing keeping this prairie from being a lake. If we were to think of Paynes Prairie as a living entity, Alachua Sink would be its beating heart.

Early Floridians knew Paynes Prairie's moods. When William Bartram explored North Florida in 1774, the local Seminole and the traders with whom he was traveling told him that the prairie, then known as Alachua Savanna, had a regular water cycle. To their credit, the Seminole also understood that Florida has an underground water system and that the prairie drains directly into it through Alachua Sink.

Surprisingly, we know little more about the vent in Alachua Sink than the Seminole knew. Logs, debris, and a healthy population of alligators have prevented Florida's famous cave divers from exploring it firsthand. But this didn't prevent the Seminole from imagining what transpired in that dark realm. According to Bartram, one prevailing belief envisioned an underground stream that flowed from Alachua Sink to the springs on the Suwannee River. This notion was bolstered in the 1820s by rumors that the corpse of a man believed to have drowned in Alachua Sink was found on the bank of the Suwannee.

Bartram, with his flair for colorful speculation, imagined an annual migration of fish that traveled great distances through the aquifer. And, like those undertaken by birds, migrations through the aquifer moved to the rhythms of the seasons. In his book *Travels*, Bartram said the prairie dried during the "latter summer season and autumn, when the powerful sunbeams have evaporated the waters off the savanna..." The fish would then "croud [*sic*] to the sink [and] descend into the earth, through the wells and cavities or vast perforations of the rocks," where they were "carried away by secret subterranean conduits and gloomy vaults, to other distant lakes and rivers." He thought that, perhaps, "In some future day, this vast savanna or lake of waters, in the winter season, will be discovered to be [filled with fish] who are strangers or adventurers from other lakes, ponds and rivers, by subterraneous rivulets and communications to this rocky door or outlet, whence they ascend to its surface, spread over and people the winter lake."

One by one, we step into our kayaks and fling the dripping slop of pennywort and hyacinth—the wrack of an ephemeral shore—off our paddles and glide onto the open water. Silently, as though drawn by some unseen force of nature—wonder, perhaps—we ease across Alachua Sink toward a large rock jutting abruptly from the water near the far edge. When exposed by lower water, this boulder has dimensions that resemble, in a way that makes me smile, a Winnebago motor home standing on end. It's an iconic feature that appears in photos dating back to the late 1800s that usually show tourists boating past or picnickers standing at its base.

The rock is skirted by a raft of water hyacinth. A bit of pushing and pulling gets me close enough to reach out and touch the cream-colored rock and move my hand over its intricately chiseled face. It feels cool and oddly damp. The sharp edges of fossilized shells and hard bits of long-extinct sea creatures dig into my fingertips. From this close perspective, I can tell this is no simple rock; it is an ossuary—every square inch of it packed with remains of sea creatures, large and microscopic, that lived and died on this spot. A geologist could read the stories told on this rock face the way an archaeologist reads petroglyphs. And in those stories she would find one simple, overarching theme—Paynes Prairie was born under the water of a shallow sea.

For millions of years of its infancy, the Florida peninsula was a submerged ridge jutting off the North American continent. The shallow sea that covered it teemed with a wild menagerie of aquatic creatures. When they died, their remains rained onto the sea floor. Modern deep-sea explorers describe a "marine snow," comprised of minute bits of decaying sea creatures that drift down incessantly to the sea floor. At times it creates an underwater white-out.

This "snow pack" of animal bits accumulated and compacted under its own weight for millions of years, forming the sedimentary rock called limestone. By the time this deposition ended, Florida's limestone platform had grown to 1,000–2,000 feet thick in places. As with its culture, the land of Florida is built upon those who lived here before.

The creatures' crunchy parts that now dig into my palm lived here thirty-five million years ago. They are from a world beyond imagining, and yet they are familiar. I see shells of Crescent Beach, periwinkles on the cordgrass of Cedar Key. I see blue-eyed scallops skipping in little jet-propelled bursts across the seagrasses of Steinhatchee.

Eventually, sea levels fell away and the limestone was freed from the salt-water of its birth. Here, in the world of light and air, it was exposed to another kind of water: rain. Most of that water evaporated, was transpired by plants, or flowed away in streams. But a small percentage percolated into the ground. This rainwater, already slightly acidic, was made more so by the decaying vegetation through which it seeped. This mildly acidic water slowly dissolved the limestone. Over vast spans of time, this process created voids in the limestone that developed into complex networks of caves and underground channels. When voids near the surface collapsed, more caves, springs, and sinkholes were formed. Large collapses created lakes and large depressions, including Paynes Prairie. It's a process that continues today, as evidenced by the cars, roads, and occasional houses that are consumed in Florida by sinkholes every year.

As I pull away from the boulder, I can see my helper, Dave, and a few others skimming past an unnaturally straight section of the sink's western shore. I've looked at that spot many times over the years, but never from this perspective, never from the water. It's a view Captain James Croxton likely had many times in the 1880s while he steered his little steam boat, the *Chacala*, toward the wooden dock that once projected into the sink at this spot. I imagine him tossing the mooring rope to workers on shore and then setting them to unloading oranges and other goods brought from groves around the lake.

The specifics are vague, but the events leading up to this chapter in the prairie's story began in 1871 when heavy rains filled the basin. Most people assumed the water would drain and the prairie would be back to its usual marshy self in a matter of weeks or months. But when the months stretched to years, it became clear something had plugged the sink. Paynes Prairie had become a lake. They called it Alachua Lake.

Contemporary accounts describe Alachua Lake as idyllically picturesque, with orange groves lining its high banks. Planters enjoyed the convenience of being able to travel and ship their produce and merchandise across the water. As the years passed and confidence in the new lake grew, the boats got steadily larger. Some started working for hire. In 1883, commercial use of the lake was ratchetted up a notch when the Alachua Steam and Navigation Company put two small steamboats into service, including the beloved *Chacala*. For almost a decade, Captains Edward Healey and James Croxton, taking turns at the helm of the *Chacala*, would come to know Alachua Lake like few people ever had in nearly fourteen thousand years of living here. Unfortunately, the navigation company ignored the one, all-important lesson of that long history: Paynes Prairie has a pulse.

In 1891, locals were reminded of the prairie's fickle nature when water levels started dropping. Whatever had plugged the sink had unplugged. By 1892, Alachua Lake was history, and Paynes Prairie was again a marsh. The *Chacala* was stranded in the muck near Bivens Arm, where it slowly decayed. Today's guests at the Paynes Prairie Preserve State Park's visitor center can see the boat's propeller, which was retrieved from the muck decades later—but I'm jumping ahead.

In the early 1900s, a phosphate company owned by Virginia timber baron William Camp purchased Paynes Prairie. The company initially planned to use it as part of a mining project. When that plan failed, they turned the prairie into a cattle ranch. It seemed like a good idea, given the prairie's lush vegetation. But once again, the prairie's dynamic hydrology was overlooked or ignored.

For the first couple of decades, the ranchers struggled to deal with wet periods. But they were untenable. In extreme high-water events, ranch workers had to temporarily relocate their cattle—sometimes as far away as Georgia.

It wasn't just the ranchers who dreamed of a drier Paynes Prairie. In 1919, and again in the mid-1920s, Alachua County citizens considered draining the prairie to make the fertile muck available for agriculture. When these proposals failed, the company took the matter into its own hands and built a system of dikes and canals.

At the same time the Camp company was building its drainage system, the state was laying the roadbed for U.S. Highway 441 across the basin. By the end of the 1920s, the Camp dikes and canals were draining nearly thirteen hundred acres of prairie basin and shunted the water directly to Alachua Sink where it drained into the aquifer. The western half of the basin was completely cut off from the eastern by U.S. 441, which acted as a dam to the slow, percolating sheet flow of water that is a vital component of the prairie's dynamic hydrology.

This was the prairie I first discovered as a kid and that would set me on a course to becoming a nature guide. Even then, in the 1960s, Paynes Prairie was known to be a critical sanctuary for wildlife. Acting on that awareness, however, has been a challenge.

The slow road to recovery began with the state's purchase of the prairie in 1971. Using Bartram's descriptions as a guide, park managers have worked to restore the prairie to its pre-settlement condition by eliminating exotic species and reintroducing some that have disappeared since Bartram's time.

In the 1990s, they broadened their efforts to include restoring the prairie's natural water cycles. But, with two highways and private properties on the low fringes of the basin, they could not completely undo Camp's drainage system. Some lesser canals were filled in and dikes removed, while others remained.

In 2009, park managers, in cooperation with Gainesville Regional Utilities and a handful of state agencies, broke ground for the most ambitious restoration endeavor to date. This multifaceted project, called the Paynes Prairie Sheetflow Project, included two primary features. One was the in-filling of the nearly two-mile Sweetwater Branch Canal that had been shunting Gainesville's runoff directly to Alachua Sink since the 1930s. The second enhancement to the prairie's hydrology was the construction of Sweetwater Wetlands Park. Situated on the north edge of the prairie, west of Alachua Sink, this 125-acre water filtration facility captures and treats urban runoff and wastewater flowing out of Gainesville via Sweetwater Branch before allowing it to flow onto the prairie. As the water flows out of these treatment cells, it slowly percolates through the vegetation and muck—further filtering out nitrogen, phosphorus, and other pollutants before being allowed to enter Alachua Sink and the aquifer.

Back at shore, we pull our boats onto solid ground in the shade of a giant live oak. With a hive of activity swirling around, a few of us talk about the trip and say goodbyes when the conversation abruptly halts with the low, rumbling bellow of a nearby alligator. We recognize the sound immediately, but in the flicker of that first instant, before my rational brain steps in, my imagination takes the reins. For just that instant, my primal mind, the one steeped in superstition and still viewing this world through the lens of a morning epiphany, hears the groan of a waking giant.

From Springs Heartland to Wasteland . . . and Back?

LUCINDA FAULKNER MERRITT

I sat upon the shore
Fishing, with the arid plain behind me
Shall I at least set my lands in order?

I first read those lines in T. S. Eliot's poem *The Waste Land* when I was very young. I read with a smattering of reverence for the poet and with a great deal of curiosity about the legend of the Fisher King that inspired Eliot, the story of a wounded king and his barren land that is part of the Holy Grail mythos. The idea that the king's wound was somehow connected with a wasted land was confusing, something I couldn't truly understand. I puzzled over it for years.

I understand it now. And it's not a myth.

. . .

My earliest memories of Florida are images of water, and throughout my life it is the springs of Florida that have magnetized and enthralled me.

The springs where I've gone swimming on hot days and cold, emerging cleansed in body, mind, and spirit—these gemlike gifts of the water gods—are but a tiny sample of the over one thousand springs that glow and sparkle throughout North Florida like earthbound stars.

I didn't know it when I was growing up in Orlando in the 1950s or when I moved to Gainesville in the mid-1960s for college—I don't think anyone knew it back then—but Florida has the largest concentration of freshwater springs in the world. Our unique landscape is not just Florida's "Springs Heartland," as one of our water management districts has dubbed it—it is the Springs Heartland of Planet Earth.

And we humans are destroying it.

. . .

Memories of my early visits to North Florida's springs are as vivid as snapshots in a photograph album. Here's one.

I am standing on the bank of Ginnie Spring in the late 1960s with my geology teacher, Jean Klein, while other members of our class—we're there on a field trip—explore different areas around the spring.

Jean and I are staring into the water. The spring is almost completely encircled by submerged aquatic plants. There is a limestone shelf that extends from below the bank out into the spring and shelters a cave below. Where the shelf ends abruptly, the color of the water changes from glass-clear to a deep Tiffany blue.

We're silent. Jean is pensive. Gazing into the spring, he muses, "You know, if this water ever gets polluted, it will take hundreds of years for Nature to clean it up."

Another time, I make my first visit to the Ichetucknee headspring with two of my college roommates. It is a year or two before Ichetucknee becomes a state park, and we're there at midafternoon on a clear, warm autumn day. Stunned by the beauty of the perfectly transparent water and amazed at our good fortune to be the only ones there, the three of us frolic in the spring, laughing and swimming and floating in the afternoon light that dapples through the surrounding trees.

Finally tired, cold, and puckered, I climb out of the spring and up a small hill to a clearing in the sun where the encircling woods are turning russet, gold, magenta. I spread out my beach towel, lie down, and shut my eyes. I relax completely in the warmth of the descending sun, drying in a soft breeze.

It isn't long before I start to hear whispering. It's leaves in the breeze, I think, unconcerned when I realize I can still hear my roommates laughing in the spring below. But after a few minutes the whispering gets louder, then louder still, until finally it resolves into words. Words in a language I've never heard.

There's someone else here, I think. I open my eyes, stand up, and turn in a full circle, carefully checking the woods around me for the strangers who are speaking this mysterious language. There is no one else there.

I wonder if I am being visited by the ancient spirits of the first people to see the Ichetucknee.

Tales of the Fisher King who guards the Holy Grail are linked to the legends of Merlin, King Arthur, and the Knights of the Round Table, parables that have always intrigued me because I sense great truths may be hidden there. Delving into these fables, I discovered that many springs throughout the British Isles were considered sacred in pagan times. Even now, Christians recognize some spring-fed wells as holy, and many communities continue the old tradition of "dressing" or decorating the wells at the solstices, equinoxes, and cross-quarter days. And people still make pilgrimages and join public gatherings at the sacred wells and springs.

This sense of the sanctity of springs isn't confined to Great Britain; it's a thread woven throughout traditional societies and different religions in cultures around the world where people continue to venerate the cherished connection that exists between humans and water.

In India and Tibet, those hallowed links are enfolded in the lore of *nagas*, animal creatures who have the lower body of a snake and the upper body of a human. *Nagas* are said to live in liminal spaces, in the unseen realms or underground in bodies of water—the ocean, springs, or lakes—or sometimes in magical trees that have exceptional power. In Buddhism, *nagas* are said to guard sacred treasure teachings that have been hidden so they may be discovered in times of greatest need.

Even here in the Springs Heartland we recognize our spiritual connection to water. I was at Rum Island Spring one day after a swim when I passed a young woman standing on the bank gazing at the water. "It's beautiful, isn't it?" I asked. Her response was immediate: "It's sacred."

At the Ichetucknee headspring, area churches have baptized the faithful for many years. One book about the Ichetucknee is subtitled "Sacred Waters." Talk to almost any spring visitor, and these ideas about the virtues of water, reverence, and rejuvenation (remember the "Fountain of Youth" legends?) crop up.

• • •

A friend came to visit me a few years ago from New York, and I took her on a tour of the springs—Rainbow, Rum Island, Ichetucknee, Manatee. It was at Manatee Spring where both of our jaws dropped.

"How beautiful!" she exclaimed. My reaction was very different: "What the hell happened here?" This was a classic example of what one of my scientist friends calls "baseline shift": my baseline, from many years ago, was the image of a clear blue spring, unsullied by green algae. My friend, who was seeing the spring for the first time, didn't realize that the green color and accompanying algae were out of place, signs of trouble not only for our springs but also for our drinking water, since both are fed by the same underground aquifer.

Ginnie Springs today is still beautiful, but the underwater plants have disappeared, possibly the result of herbicide use in the springshed.

The porous limestone aquifer in a springshed—that area of land from which groundwater feeds into a spring—is full of conduits that transport rainfall, stormwater runoff, urban and agricultural fertilizers, pesticides, and herbicides, human waste from septic tanks and wastewater spray fields, animal wastes from farms and ranches, and sewage sludge from permitted spreading areas. It does no good to point fingers or to assign greater responsibility for cleanup of pollutants to one person or another, one farm or another, because we're all to blame. We all contribute to the nitrogen, phosphorus, pesticides, herbicides, and other substances that are contaminating our freshwater springs.

The Ichetucknee, too, has changed. The river has lost about one-quarter of its historic average flow because of increased groundwater pumping, both within the springshed and from as far away as Jacksonville. The increased groundwater withdrawals are the result of population growth and intensive agricultural irrigation techniques that were introduced with center pivots in the mid-twentieth century.

Loss of flow and increased pollution have encouraged brown algae to smother green eelgrass and turned gin-clear water into murky soup. The Ichetucknee is not the same river that I first saw in the late 1960s; the changes point to an abusive relationship that we humans have with our water.

· · ·

Ginnie and Ichetucknee are not alone. Our springs—the visible top layer of the Floridan aquifer—are the "canaries in a coal mine" that warn us about problems with water quality and water supply. Long-term trends are troubling; pollution is increasing and damaging water quality, while springs throughout the Suwannee River basin have lost almost half of their historic average flows. Decreasing flows point to falling groundwater levels and problems with water supply. For every foot that freshwater in the Floridan aquifer drops, the layer of saltwater underneath rises forty feet. Once saltwater intrudes into a freshwater spring or well, there's no going back.

Every drop of water that we use is one less drop for our springs and rivers. And the same nitrate pollution that contributes to algae growth in our springs has exceeded federal safety standards in wells throughout the Springs Heartland, where freshwater in the Floridan aquifer is the sole source of drinking water for millions of people.

"Water is life," as water protectors in North Dakota and here in Florida have reminded us recently. Our bodies are up to 60 percent water. We can live about three weeks without food but only about three days without water. As water sustains us, we must in turn sustain water or suffer the consequences.

We don't need more scientific studies to tell us what is wrong because we already know. Amid enthusiastic sloganeering about the importance of jobs, economic growth, private profits, and the expenses involved in making changes, we are using too much water and permitting too much pollution. Given this knowledge, our elected representatives turn blind eyes to the problems, and state agencies charged with protecting springs continue to issue water use permits while we continue to use groundwater as an open sewer.

We need a water intervention. And myths and legends—which are often more than "just" myths and legends—can point the ways forward.

According to one of my Buddhist teachers, there are three kinds of *nagas*—benevolent, malevolent, and mutable.

When they are sickened by pollution, even the mutable and benevolent *nagas* can be angered and motivated to take revenge on the polluters. That revenge takes the form of diseases, especially skin disorders, or natural disasters. I am reminded of one of the scientists I know, a beloved elder in the springs advocacy community who can no longer swim in the springs because he's allergic to the algae that's now found there.

Whether or not you believe in the existence of *nagas*, they offer us a powerful metaphor for what we are doing here in Florida, where groundwater, springs, drinking water, and people are interconnected.

We're polluting not only the water, but also ourselves.

. . .

In the Grail legends, the barren lands of the Fisher King are directly connected to his wound. The king and his lands are both healed when the knight Perceval asks the right question: "Whom does the Grail serve?" I think the answer must have something to do with reweaving broken connections.

I have a different question for the Fisher King: where is your queen? In pagan Britain, it was a king's successful coupling with a female consort—a woman identified with the Goddess of Sovereignty—that gave the king the right to rule his people and his lands. Without joining with those qualities traditionally associated with women—empathy, sensitivity, caring, loving-kindness, compassion, nurturance, and an awareness of sacred connections—the king was unfit to rule.

It is telling that these are the same qualities that are overlooked, devalued, and even scorned in American culture and political life. That scorn and its subsequent apathy are today's manifestations of the Fisher King's raw wound. Unless we start asking the right questions, this wound will kill us as surely as it is killing our springs.

What are the questions we should be asking? Is our wound the failure to understand that as water suffers, we must suffer too? Can we heal our springs and rivers by healing our *relationships* with water and with each other? How might we create a strong water ethic? Isn't it cheaper to prevent problems than to fix them after they occur?

And where are the leaders with the courage to make the tough decisions needed to convert a Springs Waste Land back into a Springs Heartland? If our elected representatives won't help, can we meet that challenge ourselves?

. . .

I turn to the old myths and legends to create a new, healing vision for the Springs Heartland. In my vision, we reestablish our broken connections with the water and land that surround and sustain us. We collectively decide that our springs are worth saving. We come together in living rooms, libraries, churches, government offices, art galleries, and scientific laboratories to brainstorm new creative solutions for our water problems. We agree that intensive water conservation should be a primary goal before beginning costly projects that may have unintended consequences. We create a new yard aesthetic that values plant diversity and aquifer recharge over turf grass and stormwater runoff. Our agriculturalists adopt the idea of "right crop, right place," and our state agencies help farmers to adopt precision irrigation techniques. We focus on stopping pollution at its source; "thou shalt not pollute our groundwater" becomes a lived commandment. We adopt the Precautionary Principle: When in doubt about different actions that affect our environment, we choose the action that causes the least amount of harm.

We gather at the springs to observe seasonal changes and to celebrate rites of passage. In silent meditation and wonder we listen to those whispered voices on the breeze—the voices of those who came before us who can help us to understand the sanctity of the gift of clean water. We find new ways—in art, music, writing, crafts—to recognize and honor these sacred connections to water and to each other. We understand the value of reciprocity, of giving back to the water that has given us so much. We honor the myths that guide us to restore a sacred relationship with water.

We teach our children the stories of how we came together to heal the springs and each other.

As I was writing this essay, I had a phone call from my eighty-three-year-old aunt in Oklahoma. I was explaining to her why I'm trying so hard to save Florida's freshwater springs.

"We think we're separate from our environment, but we aren't," I said. "It's . . . it's. . . ." I stopped and groped for words.

Her response was better than anything I would have come up with.

"It's our home," she said.

· · ·

I sat upon the shore
Fishing, with the arid plain behind me
Shall I at least set my lands in order?

Wilderness from the Water

CLAIRE STROM

I first visited Florida in February 2008 when I flew down for an interview with the history department at Rollins College.[†] In Fargo, North Dakota, the temperature had not risen above freezing for four months, and the city was monochrome, with gray skies and asphalt framing snowy roofs and front yards. Florida, on the other hand, was having a spell of glorious weather—warm, dry, and sunny—and I was captivated by the palm trees, vibrant bougainvillea, and live oaks draped with Spanish moss. But most of all, I marveled at all the water. As my plane circled in from the Atlantic coast, I watched as Mosquito Lagoon gave way to the St. John's floodplain with rivers running every which way. Approaching Orlando, the landscape was polka-dotted with hundreds of lakes and ponds. Once on the ground, my attention turned to other things, but the impression of a land defined by water remained strong.

Six months later when I moved to Florida, I was determined to see the water. But it wasn't easy. Unlike the rivers of my English childhood, Florida rivers run through difficult terrain—marshes and thick forest—so access by foot is difficult. Lakes, too, are difficult to reach, with shorelines either privately owned or swampy. After taking a few commercial boat rides, I discovered that the inaccessibility of Florida's waterways by foot meant that, in many cases, they remain wild places, populated with myriad birds, fish, and reptiles. Thus, when

---

† My thanks to Audrey Fisch, Ginny Justice, Jim Norris, and Bob Smither for their thoughtful critiques of this piece.

my husband Jim and I bought kayaks, we opened ourselves to a whole new Florida, one dominated by nature and where we could go all day without seeing other humans.

The uniqueness of Florida's waterways starts with geology. Millions of years ago, shallow tropical seas covered the state. The life in those oceans generated sediment that compressed into limestone over vast geological periods of time. This limestone platform underlays the state and is riddled with caves and passages. The permeability of this rock, in contrast with the layers beneath, means that the limestone contains massive quantities of freshwater. This aquifer system supplies most of Florida's water, breaking through to the surface in more than seven hundred springs around the state. These crystal springs feed many of the state's rivers.

While the limestone beds developed under the ocean, the Appalachian Mountains were already above sea level. Rain falling on the mountains eroded particles, which washed south in rivers, creating sedimentary deltas on top of the Florida platform. As sea levels fell, these deltas supported a huge variety of plant and animal life, adding organic matter to the soils, developing nutrient-rich peats and marshes across the state from which emerge other Florida rivers, darker and more impenetrable than the spring streams.

Born in this blackwater, in the swamps between Interstate 95 and the Intracoastal Waterway, Bulow Creek is a short, estuarine river. The upper part of the river is a mass of cypress trees and palms, with downed trees blocking the narrow stream. As the water moves south, the creek widens into a broad sweep of salt marsh with sedge, rushes, and marsh elder lining the main river. At the edge of the Bulow flood plain, stands of huge live oak, cabbage palms, and longleaf pine provide a dense canopy above palmettos. The creek moves slowly, casting wide loops through the marsh, its edge dotted with string lilies and a burst of pink from a salt marsh morning glory. As Jim and I kayak it on a morning in late September, the sun turns the surface of the river to glassy black, but—on the white blades of my paddle—the water glows amber from tannins.

It is hot here in Central Florida, with little sign of fall, except the blue sky that presages lower humidity. Dragonflies flit over the marsh, and millions of unseen insects buzz incessantly. A pair of green herons sit in a downed tree on the water's edge and stop moving as I approach, confident in their camouflage. Meanwhile, Jim has disturbed a great blue heron, which flies away honking its disapproval. Occasionally, we hear hawks and osprey from the trees, and turkey vultures ride the thermals overhead. The black water makes it hard to see in the river, but rounding a bend, we glimpse a small alligator floating on the surface—he quickly drops below as we approach. The greatest activity this morning comes from the mullet, which are flinging themselves out of the water with abandon around our boats.

Bulow Creek is not a wilderness kayak. We can see a few houses in the trees, with docks spanning the quarter mile to the river. At the north end of the river is a small community, with modest homes scattered over a couple of canals. No one else is on the water with us, but people are fishing from docks and at our put-in at the Walter Boardman bridge. The west side of the river, however, is edged by state parks, providing a sense of wildness.

But wildness, in Florida as elsewhere, is temporal, and on Bulow Creek it masks a more complicated past. If we had kayaked this river just over two hundred years ago, we would have passed through a bustling plantation, with 2,200 acres planted in sugar cane, cotton, rice, and indigo. In 1812, the Spanish governor of East Florida, Don Juan José de Estrada, gave 2,500 acres of land to Bahamian John Russell in exchange for Russell's schooner. Russell had sailed to Florida in the schooner with his family and one hundred slaves, but he did little to develop the plantation that he named "Good Retreat" before he died in 1815. Six years later, Russell's heirs sold the land to Major Charles Bulow, who also owned a large plantation outside Charleston, South Carolina. Bulow extended the Florida holding to six thousand acres and sent down three hundred slaves to develop the estate. Bulowville, as the plantation was known, had a large, two-and-a-half-story plantation home, surrounded by a deep verandah. Around the residence were the sugar works—with a boiling house, steam engine, and sawmill—forty slave homes, a blacksmith shop, a cotton gin, a barn, and other buildings to store animals and food.

After Charles Bulow died in 1823 the plantation was managed by trustees until his son and heir, John, came of age. John, educated in Paris, took over the estate and made it a commercial success for a while and the social hub of this small community on the Atlantic coast. The plantation buildings bustled with noise and life, including the largest sugar mill in east Florida. The creek provided the route to take the produce down to the Intracoastal for transport up to the Northeast, and the plantation inhabitants used the water for washing and fishing. John also made Bulowville a center for fun for the surrounding whites, equipping an extensive library in the mansion, keeping a number of small rowboats for pleasure trips, and stocking substantial amounts of rum and ale for himself and his guests, including John James Audubon, who visited in 1831.

The settlers in the region had a good relationship with the local Seminole, who regularly provided them with meat. Therefore, in 1835 when the Second Seminole War broke out, John was not too perturbed. What did bother him, however, was the arrival in December of the Florida militia from St. Augustine, led by Major B. A. Putnam. Putnam wanted to fortify Bulowville as a base to defend the surrounding area. Bulow objected, and fired on Putnam and his men with a four-pound cannon. Bulow was arrested and taken to St. Augustine, leaving behind $28,000 worth of baled and uncleaned cotton. Putnam used the baled cotton to create a stockade around the plantation, and for a month it served as a refuge for other planters and slaves fleeing the Seminole. Finally, in late January, Putnam retreated with his forces to St. Augustine, and shortly afterward, the Seminole destroyed the plantation. The ruins remained largely untouched until purchased by the Florida Park Service in 1945. Today, these stories of steam and blood and noise are buried in the state's interpretive panels, overshadowed in all ways by the live oak canopy and the blackwater stream.

On the other side of Florida's peninsula is the Chassahowitzka River. We launch here on a cool morning in late October and kayak through dense mist, as the spring-fed water is at least 20 degrees warmer than the air. The "Chaz" is a short stream with three distinct characters. The upper river is a series of creeks spawned by springs fed from the aquifer and running through thick semi-tropical forest. The river widens out quickly, and, within a few miles, the woods thin out and are dominated by cabbage palms. These quickly give way to marsh grass through which the Chaz meanders leisurely to the Gulf.

Most of the upper Chaz is part of the Chassahowitzka National Wildlife Refuge, so we see few signs of human habitation, except for other boaters on the water. The federal government established the refugee of 30,000-plus acres of marshes, estuaries, and bays in 1943 under the Migratory Bird Act. Although originally intended to protect waterfowl, it also offers habitat to significant numbers of reptiles, mammals, aquatic life, and plants. The area has subsequently gained additional protection with various other federal and state conservation designations.

The upper river is mostly shallow and very clear. From the kayaks we can see the sandy bottom patchworked with eelgrass and bustling with fish and blue crabs. In front of the boats, small fish burst out of the water and tumble across the river in panic. On the far bank we spot the culprit as an otter disappears into the grass. A little further, two raccoons appear on a small sandy beach to watch the boats and drink. And throughout the forest the air is full of bird song.

Turning up Baird Creek toward two springs, the water narrows and the current speeds. The water is so clear and the banks so close that it is sometimes hard to know where the land begins. The rising sun sends horizontal shafts of light through the rushes to bounce off the creek in confusing prismatic glory. Live oaks and juniper reach over the water, their trunks swathed in palmetto, winterberry, and purple aster. The winding stream eventually opens into Blue Spring, a vivid splash of turquoise in the forest, and then narrows still further. Toward the head of the creek, a fallen tree blocks our kayaks, so we get out and wade fifty yards to the Crack, another, narrower, spring of brilliant blue.

Back on the main river, we kayak out of the wilderness preserve, where a few dilapidated fishing cabins dot the bank. On the opposite bank, a small commercial fishing boat that ran aground years ago is leaning drunkenly against a palm tree. Ospreys fish around us and whistle territorially at each other. Moving in closer to the bank, I see a green heron perching on a dead tree. Its neck folded in, it sits confident that its disguise as a stump is working. I get close enough to see its glossy green and maroon plumage, when the bird spooks. Its head shoots up, its body elongates, and its crest pops up like some kind of Florida Woody Woodpecker as it runs shrieking up the log.

On a neighboring branch lies a young alligator, maybe three feet long and still sporting baby stripes that help camouflage it from predators. As we pass, it rolls its body, falling into the water, six inches below. As we move further down the stream into the marsh, birdsong gives way to insect noise, and the river muddies. All around us, a great blue expanse of sky and water—glassy and still—is separated by the thinnest line of brown. The land is insignificant in this wide watery world.

Like Bulow Creek, this wilderness is temporal and elusive. Despite appearances, the area around the river has a deep human history. It was first occupied by the Weeden Island Native Americans around 1000–1300 CE. In 1528, the profoundly hapless Spanish explorer Pánfilo de Narváez and his three hundred men passed through the area searching for rich civilizations to plunder. (Narváez and many of his men later drowned while trying to return to Spanish settlements; the remaining four survivors took seven years to make their way to Mexico City.) The Seminole also knew of the river and the region, naming them both "Chassahowitzka," or "pumpkin hanging place." However, the wide expanse of swamps and broad belt of marshes lining the shore made the area difficult to traverse or settle, so, unlike Bulow Creek, it remained undeveloped until the twentieth century.

In 1910, the J. C. Turner Lumber Company built a huge lumber mill in what is now the Chassahowitzka Wildlife Management Area. The company, which originated in Michigan and also had mills in Louisiana and other parts of Florida, was interested in the expanses of virgin cypress growing in the swamps of the Chaz. Not only is cypress resistant to insects and rot, but the virgin trees were enormous, capable of supplying hundreds of board feet per tree. Specialized employees from around the world arrived to fell the trees and operate the mill. They constructed miles of railroad into the swamp. Once logs were cut, steam-powered skidders transported them to railcars that freighted them back to the mill, which was big enough to cut 100,000 board feet a day. Mules then moved the cut lumber to a drying area, as 1,000 board feet of cypress contains over three hundred gallons of water. The sun-drying took up to four years, and then the lumber was either sold or shipped through Tampa to the company's main distribution yard in New York.

A town, Centralia, emerged alongside the mill, so-called, perhaps, because one of its early inhabitants came from Centralia, Illinois. Over twelve hundred families lived in the town, making it much bigger than the county seat of Brooksville, which had only five hundred inhabitants. Centralia grew quickly, with a post office, one-room schoolhouse, hotel, church, and a movie theater called the Flicker Palace. Centralia was a company town run by the mill operator, Edgar Roberts. Roberts made sure that his employees had access to a doctor and dentist and made efforts to provide recreation, including dances. As a teetotaler, however, Roberts did not permit alcohol or saloons in Centralia—the commissary stocked soda pop instead.

Very quickly, within a decade or so, all the virgin cypress had been logged, and the mill started to cut red cedar from the swamp instead. This specialty wood was used to make pencils and cigar boxes, and it did not sustain operations for long. The mill closed before 1920, and the town was abandoned by 1922. The Turner Company continued to own the land, however, and in the 1960s planted much of it with slash pine. That operation came to an end in 1985 when the Florida Fish and Wildlife Conservation Commission purchased the land.

The historian in me loves the cognitive dissonance. Floating past an alligator just off the dock where Bulowville stood, I imagine the stink of the processing sugar and the mounds of fermenting indigo leaves. Jim and I wave at an African American family from Sanford fishing in their favorite spot, where a century before hundreds of slaves had toiled loading cotton bales on flatboats for transport out to the St. Johns. Similarly, in the tangled wilderness of the Chaz, I think about the deep scars cut by huge cypress falling through the forest, the piercing shriek of a train whistle, and the never-ending racket of the massive sawmill blades. My paddles through Florida waterways expose the state's raw natural beauty, but that same beauty elides a complicated past of settlement, deforestation, industrialization, and slavery. Finding my way into the inaccessible, wet heart of Florida, I have also discovered those obscured histories that lie beneath and around the water.

The Rhythms of the Lagoon

CLAY HENDERSON

In my selective memory is a color-coded sequence to a perfect dawn on the lagoon. It begins in the pre-dawn blackness where water and sky meet and light from the heavens reflects off still waters. First light reveals dark silhouettes of sabal palms along the subtropical shore and the movement of night herons heading for their daytime roost. A deep crimson glow next emerges above and then across the water accented by white streaks across the sky. Red dissolves into orange as the upper limb of the sun inches above the horizon, a spark that triggers ripples from under the water and soon fills the air with white, blue, and pink wings. The lagoon is waking up. Pure yellow light pours across the water, transforming the hue of the lagoon waters from blue to green as the penetrating light exposes the vast underwater rainforest beneath. So many times I've said to myself or a close friend that this is my favorite place on earth. All this unfolds from the stage of a poling platform, gliding along the flat reflective waters of Mosquito Lagoon in its stillness and quiet just before someone exclaims, "Fish On!"

For most of my life, I have lived in close proximity to the Indian River Lagoon. Growing up, most of my friends answered the call of surf and waves, but I was a self-proclaimed river rat. The waters of the lagoon run through my veins and the air that I breathe is laced with salt. Protection of the lagoon is personal to me.

Some earliest memories are connected to the lagoon. I remember as if it were yesterday something that happened six decades before. While wading the shallow waters of the lagoon near the confluence with Spruce Creek, my dad bent over and plucked an oyster from the sandy bottom. He opened the shell with his Barlow jackknife and separated the live mollusk from its shell. Then he handed me the shellfish and said, "try this." I still remember how salty it tasted, just as I recall the joys of seeing my first dolphin and first manatee and roseate spoonbill.

We always called this body of water "the river," but it is really an estuary. While it looks like a river, it has a very different ebb and flow. For those of us who live near an inlet, the river flows north for six hours, then slows to slack, and then smoothly reverses course and flows back south for the next six hours. The hands of nature's master clock register four tides each day every six hours, over a twenty-four-hour day. The following day, all of this repeats, though approximately one hour later. Seven days later, the tides will be opposite of the first day, and fourteen days later, they will be the same. It is a predictable rhythm in a four-part symphony that is different every day.

At some point we learned that our river was technically a lagoon, or a shallow estuary separated from the sea by a narrow barrier island. Estuaries and lagoons are a special brackish mixing zone of the freshwaters from the interior of the peninsula and the ocean waters of the Atlantic. Estuaries are among the richest habitats on the planet, and this one is no different. This 156-mile estuary is especially significant because it is the only one to span both the tropical and temperate climatic zones. Scientists debate whether it is in fact the most biologically diverse, but no one has been able to prove otherwise. Dr. Duane DeFreese, who has been studying and protecting the lagoon for three decades, says, "The Indian River Lagoon ecosystem is one of the great estuarine ecosystems in North America." What we do know is that thousands of species call the Indian River Lagoon home, and many more pass through it as part of the extraordinary migratory patterns of sea and air that span the hemisphere. Scientists have documented over four thousand species, including two thousand plant, six hundred fish, and three hundred bird species. However, it is equally important to note that fifty species are formally listed under the federal Endangered Species Act as either endangered, threatened, or special concern. An example is the Atlantic salt marsh snake. The official listing notes that "its population level is currently unknown" because so few are left. There are other species whose numbers are in steep decline but not yet in the queue of formal listing. American oystercatchers, with their distinctive red-orange eyes and bills, were a common sight in my youth but now are hard to come by.

Humans have lived along the Indian River Lagoon for millennia. Shell middens such as Turtle Mound, Castle Windy, Ross Hammock, and Seminole Rest are visible reminders of native people who gathered fish and shellfish along the rich waters of the lagoon as far back as two thousand years ago. The discovery of Windover Archaeological Site in Titusville provided proof of human settlement back to 5000–6000 BC. A century ago, archaeologists in Indian River County discovered *Vero Man*, who may have lived along the lagoon some twelve thousand years ago.

Europeanized place names associated with the lagoon are among the oldest in the Americas. The Alberto Cantino map of 1502 lists *Cabo Cañareal*, or what we now call Cape Canaveral. It may be the oldest American place name appearing on a map a mere decade after Columbus's first voyage. In 1513, Juan Ponce de León named the peninsula *la Florida*, and the inlet that now bears his name was described as *Rio los Mosquitos*, or Mosquito River. As Spaniards settled Florida, Álvaro Mexía was dispatched south along the peninsula to map their new territory. South of Canaveral, Mexía interacted with the native Ais people who lived along the lagoon. They called themselves the *people of the river*, and likewise called the water the *river of the people*. Mexía's 1605 map translated that as *Rio de Ais*. Centuries later, the name was Anglicized as Indian River. Mexía's map also correctly identified that the lagoon consisted of three segments, including what we now call Indian River, Mosquito Lagoon, and the Banana River.

One of the legacies of the Spanish were the scurvy-fighting oranges they left behind to take root along the lagoon. When colonial naturalist William Bartram surveyed the New Smyrna Colony in 1774, he described the coastal hammock as a vast orange grove. But these wild Spanish oranges grew fruit with a remarkably sour taste. In the mid-nineteenth century, Douglas Dummett perfected grafting buds from sweet orange plantings to the old Spanish stock. Once Henry Flagler's railroad was completed through the Indian River area by 1892, fresh fruit from Indian River groves could arrive via rail to New York in just a few days. After that, "Indian River Fruit" became world famous.

Flagler's railroad transformed Florida and life along the Indian River. His coastal resorts attracted regular visitors who fished the rich waters of the lagoon and came under the spell of tropical South Florida. Over the span of a century, the Florida peninsula was transformed from a mosquito-infested backwater to the nation's third largest state. Beginning in the 1960s, millions of residents and visitors stood along the shores of the lagoon to watch astronauts launched into space from Cape Canaveral, bringing world attention to the area. Today, nearly two million people live within the watershed of the lagoon.

Within the history of the lagoon are the roots of the modern conservation movement. Early naturalists Bartram and André Michaux first chronicled flora and fauna along the lagoon. Indeed, it was Bartram who first confirmed that Florida was a place where northern birds disappeared to for the winter. A century later, many of the wading birds he described were on the brink of extinction. This led to an awakening of people interested in conservation who founded Florida Audubon Society in 1900. Frank Chapman, curator of the American Museum of Natural History, and Audubon members urged President Theodore Roosevelt to designate Pelican Island, a rookery in the Indian River near Sebastian Inlet, as America's first wildlife refuge in 1903. Today, Pelican Island, Merritt Island, Archie Carr, and the newly designated Nathaniel Reed National Wildlife Refuges protect those wading birds and important lagoon habitat.

Florida's progression from a subtropical wilderness to a vibrant urban state placed all of our natural resources under stress. In the decades prior to the passage of the 1972 Clean Water Act, untreated wastewater poured into those once gin-clear waters of the lagoon. For much of this same period the vast mangrove forests of the lagoon were ditched, drained, and sprayed with pesticides for mosquito control. Nearly 80 percent of Florida's population lives within twenty miles of the coast, and none of our coastal cities could have been built without draining the proverbial swamp. Even today, over a quarter-million people in the lagoon watershed live in houses with septic tanks. Nutrients from septic tanks, stormwater discharges, and wastewater treatment contribute to the slow decline of a natural wonder.

Much of the problem is plumbing. Canals that drained our cities and opened more land for citrus more than doubled the watershed and increased the quality and quantity of freshwater entering the lagoon. Manmade inlets added connections to the ocean that increased salinity and tides in places where the water was less brackish, and tides were driven by wind instead. Other canals linked the lagoon to both Lake Okeechobee and the St. Johns River, which made unnatural hydrological connections to different kinds of pollution sources. Each of these changes altered the natural mixing of fresh interior water and ocean sea salts.

By the 1980s, the lagoon started showing significant signs of stress. In 1983, educator/activist Diane Barile formed the Marine Resources Council to draw attention to its plight. In 1989, the group organized "hands across the lagoon," with hundreds of volunteers forming a human chain across bridges that spanned the waterway. It was a plea for help, and President George H. W.

Bush answered the call. Bush, whose parents kept a house on Jupiter Island, was familiar with the area, and on Earth Day 1990 he interrupted a fishing trip in Florida Bay to announce the Indian River Lagoon as an Estuary of National Significance. This led to its induction into the National Estuary Program, with the benefits of national and state attention. Tallahassee responded as well with passage of the Indian River Lagoon Act, which improved wastewater treatment and focused local government on water re-use. During the next ten years, the lagoon's water quality actually improved.

Over the next twenty years, there was a prevailing feeling that the lagoon was improving, and attention turned to other issues, but in 2011 a perfect storm wreaked havoc. A brown algae previously unknown to Florida took hold and choked out the sunlight necessary to sustain the vast lagoon seagrass beds. That summer, thousands of acres of seagrasses died, with extensive mortalities to dolphins, manatee, and pelicans.

I've never felt so helpless watching the slow-motion decline of the Indian River Lagoon. It was like watching my mother die all over again. She died in 2005 following a ten-year decline from Alzheimer's disease. Her first symptoms included senility, as she happily recalled camping along the magical banks of the lagoon in the family's new 1927 Model A Ford. Over time, we watched her fail in a stair-step process in which she would be stable for a while and then drop to the next stage of decline without warning until the end. During the height of the algae bloom, I paddled out of Haulover to inspect one of the lagoon's largest rookeries to check its health. Along the way, I saw a massive redfish breaking through the opaque pea soup waters to catch a breath of air while dead fish floated nearby. The last breath of all living creatures looks much the same.

For a while the lagoon appeared to be on the mend. The brown tide dissipated, sea grasses started to rebound, and fishing guides happily reported good catches of the lagoon's signature species of seatrout and redfish. Unfortunately, this period of resilience was all too brief. In January 2016, we were all surprised to see a return of algae blooms far earlier in the season than ever before. Blue-green algae was the first to bloom, followed by the return of brown algae. By February, algae blooms affected the entire Indian River Lagoon, such that photographs from satellites in space showed the signature pea-soup tint of the bloom. By mid-March, a massive fish-kill erupted in the central portions of the lagoon near Merritt Island. By some accounts, more than a million fish died, and over 100,000 pounds of dead fish were removed. The governor declared a state of emergency in the wake of an environmental crisis.

Citizens up and down the coast responded to the call for help. Some blamed discharges from Lake Okeechobee, while others blamed septic tanks. From Washington, D.C., to Tallahassee to local county commissions, interest was renewed in fixing the lagoon. Brevard County took up the challenge, and voters approved a $300 million bond issue to undertake protections designed to restore the lagoon. Congress and the Florida legislature authorized major projects to halt the flow of nutrient-laden waters from Lake Okeechobee.

In December 2018, representatives of public agencies and stakeholders transmitted to the U.S. Environmental Protection Agency (EPA) a restoration plan for the Indian River Lagoon. The plan is not perfect, but all the ingredients are there to further science, monitoring, adaptive management, and projects, which total well over $1 billion. The plan was accepted by acclamation and with a sense of urgency because we must get started on lagoon restoration and recognize that it won't happen overnight.

Restoration for me has always been about restoring hope that an ecosystem will thrive once again. The difficulty here is defining the goals of restoration, since practically we can't close manmade inlets and return the lagoon to a primordial beauty known only to the Ais. But we do know that the lagoon is incredibly resilient. It responds to multiple stressors and dynamics and has demonstrated an ability to rebound. The lagoon also provides essential ecosystem services for people and wildlife. For me, restoration of the lagoon looks like a body of water that is stable and clean enough to sustain fish and shellfish populations and migratory birds while providing essential ecosystem services that we all can enjoy.

Late each summer I return to a special area around Haulover Canal across a narrow isthmus that separates Mosquito Lagoon from the Indian River. On moonless nights, it is as if a celestial switch has flipped, and the rhythms of the lagoon reveal an eerie greenish light called bioluminescence. Tiny dinoflagellate plankton that emit low levels of light when disturbed is the source of the light. When millions of plankton are disturbed in unison, it is enough to light the way of a kayak on an otherwise dark night and reveal the magic of the lagoon. Jumping mullet become neon streaks of light. Dayglow dolphins break the surface tension of the water to catch their breath. Ghostly manatees glow as they sleep beneath the calm waters. Charles Darwin once described bioluminescence as "a wonderful and most beautiful spectacle," but in essence it is living light.

I return to these waters each summer, along with many others. We call the lagoon our own fountain of youth. For a couple of hours each night, we can literally bathe in the living waters of the lagoon, dipping our hands into the magical water, watching it glow in living light. Everyone who spends a summer night like this ends up giggling like a teenager.

When the lagoon gives its living light, it conveys to us a message of hope. If enough of us care, we can bring back the Indian River Lagoon to a healthy condition. It is resilient, and we need to be as well.

Raw Water

GIANNA RUSSO

Hillsborough River
Her birthplace is the Green Swamp.
Withlacoochee, Ocklawaha, and Peace are her sisters.

She flows for miles like a singing highway, then forks
into almost twenty wet fingers with names
like Big Ditch, Flint Creek, Moon Lake.
For centuries we've worried her banks,
left behind arrowheads and teacups,
picked bones, garbage pits.
Narváez inspected her shores, then deSoto.
We banished or killed her birthright tribes.
Now Zephyrhills bottles her headspring waters.

She's a blackwater river stained dark brown by nature.
Her cool, raw water is Tampa's fountain
and the quality's good, but for occasional
arsenic, nitrate, phosphate and lead,
gasoline, pesticides, herbicides, oil and all
old medicines flushed down the drain.

These are her living creatures:
bobcat, egret, wood stork, osprey,
alligator, river otter, blue heron, ibis,
raccoon, water snake and great bald eagle.
On her banks, I've seen lovers pledge their *I Do's*,
then row away in a daisy-draped boat.
Floating her canoe trails, no one can judge you.

Before ever I grew breasts
my grandmother would pack pimento cheese
and walk us to the end of my street
where the river trundled off like a slow roving horse
and ambled towards the city.
We had cane poles and chicken necks.
There we stood in front of folding chairs,
as tannic water doubled back
and mullet jumped into the brackish.

She was called the Mocoso,
the Lockcha-Popka-Chiska.
Crazy Life river, you might want to name her.
River where loss turns up like potsherds
and joy flashes over her rapids.
Her bye-gones and goodbyes are all brown froth.

Her daughter is open water.
Her mother, the Green Swamp.

PART V

TERRA FIRMA

Excerpts from *The Galley*

MARJORY STONEMAN DOUGLAS

Miami Herald, June 23, 1923[*]

There is really nothing more invigorating and thrilling than to ride far out into the Everglades, or into the edge of them, and watch the clouds piling high in great soft-toned mountains, over the wide expanse of lavish green earth which opens out on every hand clear to the sharp cut rim of the horizon. With all these rains the greens of tall grass and of crop-land are brilliant, jewel-like. There are thousands of small, half-hidden flowers, purple and soft blue and mustard yellow, woven in with the green and under the driving wind the clouds leave great cracks and clefts for the full dazzle of the sunlight to cut through in great rays and streaks, leaving even more brilliant patches of sun moving across the vast surface of the green. All the little insects are loud in the grass in the sunshine, or, if you are there toward the end of the afternoon when the sunset which will presently blazon not just the west with burning, molten gold, but the clouds with white and rosy lights, and the east with the pink, is generally imminent, the air will be filled with the quick, circling flight of the whippoorwills, or bull-bats, lifting on sharp, white-barred wings to different air levels and supplying the whole of the sky with silent motion. It is quiet out there, except for these small sounds of insects or rustling grass, that it seems that if one could be still

---

[*] For three years in the 1920s, Marjory Stoneman Douglas wrote a daily column for the *Miami Herald* she called "The Galley."

enough, and long enough, that some tremendous meaning that is behind this silence would be made known. Or the purpose of the tremendous winds which move and start and come forward or change direction and go roaring away to some other horizon, as if they were the presence of some great being, playful and unwatched here on their vast hearthstone.

Miami Herald, December 3, 1922

It was our privilege a little before twilight an afternoon recently, to be taken to see one of the oldest places in Coconut Grove, which has never been manicured by a landscape gardener or cleared from its original planning since the first, but which has recently gone on growing during the drums and tramplings of a thousand real estate men beyond its gates, a bit of old South Florida, as lovely, as remote, as anything in the South Sea isles. You enter by a gate which is just another of those gates along that mellow Coconut Grove road. Beyond that the path winds and twists slowly, plunging you almost at once in a jungle growth which almost meets over your head. Huge Caribbean pine trees dispute the way of the jungle at first, but their place is taken by enormous gumbo limbo, by live oaks, by a dark feathery jacaranda and countless other shrubs and trees and creepers, making a green gloom of the fading light. Your footsteps are silent on dark soft earth and you go softly, too, hushed. The clearing opens beyond the path end with a wide lawn of rank soft grass which has not been cut, but allowed to grow free right to the steps of the house, a huge dark brown shape in the surroundings. Far down the slope that leads to the far glimpses of the bay there are other great Caribbean pines, enormous, mysterious, the true pine of South Florida, hoary as if forgotten survivals from sea. Down the grassy slope, the path slips silently through air brown with the luminousness of twilight, down to the levels of palms and black shaggy masses of bamboo. But you hardly notice those at first, for starlight beyond, as lofty, as permanent, as granite, as some pillars move two rows of royal palms, reaching in utter majesty out to the afterglow of sunset, fit altar for their tremendous cathedral. Through all this there is not the slightest sound. You stand gazing, in silence, wholly in reverence. It is a cathedral which needs no incense nor requires worshippers. But when you turn, the sunset is a blaze of flat gold behind the huge pines on the hill, and you know that this dimness, this immense green, is the very secret place of old South Florida, for which there were never any Druids, elemental, mysterious, hoary, but young with the youth of all the world, of all growth, of all life. It is a very wonderful thing to have been allowed to tiptoe over its threshold.

Miami Herald, December 20, 1921

Look out your window. Can you see a pine tree? If you can, you're lucky. They are going fast. And every day somebody cuts down a few more to make a new subdivision that, without them, will be as raw and ugly as plain dirt without trees can be. Do you own a pine tree? Then you are lucky. But if you appreciate it, you are more than that. You have a genuine eye for beauty, which is another word for spiritual common-sense.

The Natural Aesthetic of the Naked God

BRUCE STEPHENSON

I experience the wild heart of Florida on a brisk day hiking an unmarked trail in the Lake Wales Ridge State Forest. Finding this xeric haven required study. Examining satellite images, I found a line of white fingers—the remains of ancient sand dunes—that thread Walk-In-The-Water Wilderness Management Area (named for a nearby lake). Seven million years ago, this spate of rare uplands was part of the thin strip of peninsular Florida standing above the primal seas. Evolving in isolation, the Lake Wales Forest has one of the highest concentrations of rare and endangered species in the continental United States. Walk-In-The-Water is also a topographical wonder. In the nation's lowest lying state, its strand of sandy ridges resembles an Old Testament wilderness. The ideal place to, as John Muir put it, "touch the naked god."

Accessible only by foot, the scrubby desert environs are purified by fire. Fires burn every one to three years, and their residue provides nutrients for new growth. Yet, the habitat stays sparse with a limited plant palette. Thus, a basic botanical knowledge allows me to glean the clues to navigate the property. Bound to nature, I ignore marked trails and follow deer tracks and my intuition. After twenty-odd trips to Walk-in-the-Water, "The path will reveal itself," is my mantra. A bad day is measured by time spent in a rutted manmade trail, and away from the organic grace the fire-cleansed wilderness offers.

I plan my pilgrimage to coincide with a cool day, ideally in the 40s at sunrise. The reflected heat from the site's white sands adds to the temperature, which makes the hike insufferable most of the year. I begin scouting for the right day after Thanksgiving, and my first trek falls on the edge of the winter solstice. As the day approaches, I am filled with the giddiness of a childhood Christmas Eve. The gift is jettisoning the invasive digital overload of modern life to meditate in wildness and ponder the untouched parts of the land, and of my soul.

Rising early, I pass through the sprawling, paved mediocrity of metropolitan Orlando in darkness. The streaks of a lavender-peach sunrise unveil a picturesque expanse of orange groves that denotes the destination is close at hand. Upon arriving, I cannot extricate myself from the rented vehicle quick enough (I do not own a car). Crossing into the forest, I feel an immediate rush of energy. Adult restraint morphs into boyish enthusiasm and, spotting a deer path, I break into a fast-paced gait and immerse myself in the sights, sounds, smells, and textures. After fifteen minutes, the trail gives out in a circle of white sand surrounded by the tight formation of myrtle oaks and sand live oaks that dominate the lower elevations. Having accustomed myself to the surroundings, I am not too alarmed and scour the area for clues to reach the ridges.

A longleaf pine appears in the immediate distance. The forest's dominant species, the shade-intolerant tree can grow to one hundred feet tall. Its needles, which reach eighteen inches, give the fire-resistant species its name. Its rough, flaky bark and lower limbs burn away in the frequent fires, but the living tissue survives. The tree can live over three hundred years, but its gestation is slow. It takes seven years for the taproot, which extends up to twelve feet, to reach the water table and nourish the species. During this period, the tree has a grass form and looks much like wiregrass, another pyrogenic species. But it is the turkey oak, a deciduous drought-tolerant tree that is my guide.

Longleaf pine, turkey oak, and wiregrass are commonly found in sandhill habitats. Walk-in-the Water is designated a scrub ecosystem, but its highest elevations are dominated by these three sandhill species that support a rich colony of gopher tortoises. Turkey oaks stand as high as fifty feet, but most of the species are much smaller, as fires keep them stunted and scattered, especially away from the ridges. Spaced in a less congested manner than the other scrubby oaks, a hiker can skirt turkey oaks without having to "bushwhack." In late December, their leaves are rustic red and easy to spot, and a string of them aligned with a longleaf pine is the avenue to the higher elevations that lead to the ridges.

The other challenge is finding a bridge of land to cross the wetland strands that bisect the site. Up to a quarter mile long, in the early morning sun they resemble the savannahs that birthed the first human tribes. The brown waving grasses have an amber hue, and their faint rustling is punctuated by a sand-hill crane's occasional squawk. Bordered by chalky bluestem grass and dense stands of palmettos, I hug the wetland's edge until sighting a narrow bridge of land centered on a mature sand live oak. Passage is easy under the tree's spread of limbs, and I reach a patch of oak scrub at a slightly higher elevation. After four such crossings, the first ridge appears.

As I emerge through a ring of palmettos, the habitat changes as the small burnt-orange leaf of the blueberry bush bleeds into a pile of rusty brown pine needles indented by the large cones of the longleaf pine. The elevation steepens, and openings of white sand appear marked by deer and, I like to think, bobcat prints. Trailing higher, the S-shaped mark of the endangered sand sink appears. Its trace is a careful carving for a Zen garden shaped by nature.

No gardener could match the congruent randomness of the plant placement and coloring of these xeric enclaves. Pink and white wireweed mix with splays of yellow-green gopher apple. This hardy shrub spreads through a matrix of underground stems and, with its short stature and leathery oblong leaves, a run of gopher apple takes the form of a school of fish intent on reaching the ridge top. Other treats capture the eye as well. Yellow button flowers pair with the olive-green leaves of sky-blue lupine, a mix highlighted by wiregrass's brown-green stems. A smattering of woody-stemmed beargrass outlines a mass of deer moss, puffy pale greenish-gray lichens that glow white in the bright sun. A sign of good air quality, according to woodsman's lore. I breathe in reams of oxygen through the world's most natural filter, a long-standing forest.

My lungs refreshed, I continue the ascent and catch the sparkle of a Garberia's efflorescent purple flower. The evergreen shrub pairs with a prickly pear, which has a narrow tubular flower of a similar tint. When hiking with a companion, encountering a prickly pear requires a shout out because its needles can pierce a hiking boot with the precision of a ninja assassin. A resilient species, the cactus is a reminder of the unique xeric landscape within a rain-sodden region.

Polk County receives fifty-two inches of rain per year. Over 80 percent falls during hurricane season, and the water drains rapidly through the sandy soil to replenish the aquifer—Florida's primary source of potable water. Scrub habitat is rare, but it is endangered because this floodless land is ideal for development in a state where flood insurance is sold at a premium. Of course, subdivisions and strip malls do not replenish aquifers, protect biodiversity, or allow wildlife movement. Yet, the human habitat does not have to be a resource sink.

Orlando's supply of potable water is quickly diminishing, largely because 50 percent of it goes to lawn irrigation. Native landscaping can mitigate this problem. To demonstrate this option, in 2005, my students and I planted a native garden in a former sandhill section of Winter Park's Central Park. We wanted to reveal what author-ecologist Aldo Leopold called a "natural aesthetic," the beauty that native plants provide in their form and function. In the intervening years, Walk-In-The-Water has informed the plans for the garden's expansion. Today, the garden's longleaf pines top the park's live oaks, while a cohesive understory of gopher apple, blueberry, myrtle and turkey oak, beargrass, palmetto, and juvenile pines hint at Florida's wild heart.

To fathom its beat, however, I saunter across the Lake Wales Ridge in search of the naked god. Over two hundred feet in height, the ridges in Walk-in-the-Water are among the highest points on the Florida peninsula. Reaching a ridge top on the edge of the winter solstice, a cloudless cerulean sky is the backdrop for an unmatched view of unbroken wildness. In the foreground, forest-green palmettos and white sugary sand underscore a phalanx of small turkey oaks impersonating their Vermont relatives. Awash in golden yellows and reds, the oaks blend into a stand of longleaf pine a football field away. In the far distance, the flat crown of an ancient pine tops another ridge, a sign that the forest dates to a time when Florida was a Gilded Age backwater, the least populated state east of the Mississippi and of little interest to anyone, particularly national politicians.

Even on a cool day the ridge top is warm. Finding relief in the fractured shade of a longleaf pine, I cushion myself in a bed of needles. A high-decibel truncated squeal couples with a brilliant white flash to announce a bald eagle's presence. Following its looping, spherical flight sets the rhythm for deciphering hints of the divine. "Nature is too thin a screen," Transcendentalist author Ralph Waldo Emerson wrote: "the glory of the omnipresent God bursts through everywhere." Comforted and comfortable in my space, I notice that the pine boughs overhead form perfect circles, the figure Leonardo Da Vinci drew to reveal his genius. Nature's perfect form is welcoming as well. A light breeze moves the pine needles as delicate as an Audrey Hepburn wave in a vintage film. A gust of wind intensifies the greeting, and the tree shimmies like a dance troupe fluttering fans in unison. The lively crew of neighboring conifers, ranging from juveniles to the aged, joins in, and I revel in our communion.

Like us, our arboreal relatives are relational beings. They thrive in communities and work together to nurture growth, fight off disease, and produce life's most beneficial products: clean air and water. Approximately 1.5 billion years ago the arboreal gene pool branched out, setting the path for our species evolution. Today, humans and trees share 25 percent of the same genes, and the survival of both species depends on their communal instinct.

Genes are passed through individuals, but human evolution is predicated on forming complex groups. Thus, the brain is wired in two basic ways: individuals focus on either immediate self-interest, or they think in a more reflective and rational manner about how to improve their common welfare. These impulses are in perpetual conflict and theologians, not surprisingly, argue that religion is intrinsic to survival because it translates our propensity for altruism into ritual.

In the United States, the preeminence of civic religion gave birth to a special relationship between God and nature. In the opening paragraph of the Declaration of Independence, Thomas Jefferson called upon fellow colonists to form a new nation "which the Laws of Nature and Nature's God entitle them." The rejection of divine rule and religious superstition defined the radicalism of the American Revolution, and the founding fathers' deism—-the belief that the laws of nature held rational truths to guide a free people and bring them closer to nature's God. With the advent of the Industrial Revolution, nature became a point of worship as well as study. Decrying that "Things are in the saddle they ride mankind," Emerson in the nineteenth century found in nature a "sanctity that shames our religions." Inspired by this Concord sage, author John Muir took his adage to its logical conclusion and cofounded the Sierra Club for "the thousands of tired, nerve shaken, over civilized people beginning to find wildness is a necessity."

More than a century later, Americans are increasingly finding spiritual meaning in nature. At the same time, Yahweh, the Old Testament god, is making a comeback. It was on the outskirts of the Fertile Crescent, in an environment not unlike the Lake Wales Ridge, where the Hebrew tribes encountered the ancient patriarch deity: a jealous god who threatened the decadent kingdoms populating the verdant river valleys of Mesopotamia. As we burn through our resources at a rate that imperils future generations, Yahweh embodies the day of reckoning climate change portends. "Fire goes before him and consumes his foes on every side," the psalmist averred. It is this existential threat Pope Francis seeks to remedy in his encyclia, *Our Common Home* (2015). Calling for investments in "smart growth," he writes, "We need to think of containing growth by setting some reasonable limits, and even retracing our steps before it is too late."

The poster child of unrestrained growth, Florida is in peril. Its voracious appetite for development feeds on uplands, which has turned the state's remnant xeric systems into artifacts, accounting for only 4 percent of the historic total. Even more alarming, Florida's unique system of land and water has been engineered into the backdrop for suburbia. Awash in toxic algae, red tide, and saltwater intrusion, this specter is matched by the state's mechanized death. In road-rage-riveted metropolitan Orlando, a driving fatality occurs every forty-four hours, pedestrians are impaled weekly, and bicyclists die at an equally foreboding rate. Yet, Orlando is not forsaken. In fact, the city just may offer a path to the Promised Land.

In 2005, a University of Pennsylvania study determined that Central Florida could accommodate seven million people and sustain ecological health by constructing an integrated transportation system (rail, bus, and streetcar) to support a denser, more compact development pattern. In addition, state and local government needed to acquire the remaining links to complete the region's ring of nature preserves. The good news is that smart growth centers Orlando's new *Greenworks Plan* (2018), which has the goal of making the city "resilient to the impacts of climate change." The state legislature has also stepped up, appropriating monies to jumpstart natural lands acquisition. In the two decades before the Great Recession, state purchases set the foundation for encircling metropolitan Orlando with green. The Lake Wales Ridge Forest is key to this initiative, and deft political leadership could bring it to fruition.

The forest's very existence emboldens my hopes for a sustainable future. It is not only ecologically rare, it offers enlightenment. "At the gates of the forest," Emerson wrote, "the surprised man of the world is forced to leave the city estimates of great and small, wise and foolish." Here one fathoms why building communities patterned on a life-giving forest follows the laws of nature. Moreover, human survival is predicated on the species being a moral animal and, with the catastrophe of climate change imminent, placing limits on growth conveys our reverence to nature's god. Fortunately, aligning ourselves with nature is endemic to the American experience, and tapping into nature's wild heart is an instinctual celebration of life. The antidote to the cacophonic consumerism that prices our lives and steals the soul, touching the Naked God is an act that marks my path to salvation.

Don't Mourn the Orange

MARK JEROME WALTERS

My house sits on what was once the wildest spot in North America.

So does yours.

Half a millennium ago, magnificent high pine and scrub grew on the ancient sand-ridge where our neighborhood now stands in St. Petersburg, Florida. You don't need to be a geologist or archeologist to excavate this deep past. An ant will do.

The small Kilimanjaros of tawny sand that ants leave along our brick street speak of the ancient history. Some soil experts say the color and composition of the ant hills suggest that high pine forests and scrub may have dominated this area of Pinellas County. For thousands of years before Europeans arrived, red cockaded woodpeckers flew through shadows among columns of tree trucks the girth of mule bellies. These were tall, massive trees that created the aura romantics would later call cathedral forests—places where humans felt overwhelmed by stillness and grandeur. Of these pines, one visitor in the mid-1800s wrote, "There was something, I thought, very graceful in the millions upon millions of tall and slender columns, growing up in solitude, not crowded upon one another, but gradually appearing to come closer and closer, till they formed a compact mass, beyond which nothing was to be seen."

Often growing next to areas of longleaf pine were patches of evergreen oak shrubs and tough, drought-resistant plants known collectively as scrub. Long-leaf pine was majestic, shadowy and high. Scrub was short, sunny and hot. High pine, or yellow long-leaf, dominated the Atlantic coastal plain of the southeastern United States; scrub lived almost nowhere outside Florida. The most distinctive resident of the scrub was the Florida scrub-jay, a long-tailed bird with scintillating blue feathers. Fearful of hawks lurking in the high canopy of the longleaf, the scrub-jays rarely crossed the distinct boundary between sunlight and shadow.

Although opposite in stature, the scrub and longleaf pine were ecological brethren. They both grew on well-drained sand ridges, and they both needed periodic fires for maintenance. Although the habitats were different at any moment, they could be one in the same over time: if scrub got burned too often, it would eventually give itself to longleaf pine. This was the ancient, interconnected pattern of pine and scrub that may have once occupied the upland ridges in the part of the county where our neighborhood now stands.

The houses sit atop the remnants of ancient dunes about thirty feet above current sea level. Just don't expect a view. These ridges marking former coastlines are greatly worn down. And keep in mind that hills in Florida are usually measured in millimeters. You never know when you're walking up one. The sand the ants mine from four or five feet beneath the bricks was deposited by winds, waves, and ocean currents when the Gulf of Mexico covered the area off and on over millions of years. As sea level retreated, the dunes remained. Since their formation, sea level has fallen so much that our house is now six miles from the Gulf of Mexico.

This picture of the neighborhood's ancient past isn't just creative speculation. In the early 2000s, several geographers analyzed soil types throughout Pinellas County to determine the location of the "historic xeric uplands." This is the fancy name for places with very dry, deep, and well-drained hills of sand favored by high pine and scrub, as well as by some hardwood hammocks. Our neighborhood sits right smack in these historic "uplands."

High pine and scrub may have covered our neighborhood for perhaps eight thousand years before the coming of settlers. It survived the indigenous Tocobaga and Spanish, French, and English settlers. The high pine survived the toiling hand-saw of the early 1800s. But the valuable forests wouldn't outlive the steam-age, which brought railroads and machines to haul the felled behemoths from deep within forests to the rivers that carried them to steam-driven mills. The high pine in Pinellas County was almost certainly gone by the late 1800s, but much of the "useless" scrub survived newer waves of settlement, the modern loggers, the ranchers, and the farmers. But by the early 1900s, the throw-away scrub—or, rather, the land beneath it—had begun to turn gold.

Which brings me to the subject of oranges.

In 1912, Mary Eaton, a wealthy resident of St. Petersburg, planted an orange grove on the very block where our house now stands. She watered her grove during dry periods by pumping thousands of gallons of groundwater through a circuit-board of ditches among the trees. Workers poured fertilizer around the base of the trees. They sprayed the leaves with pesticides. Eaton was part of an agricultural upheaval that was changing the landscape of Florida and, in the process, helping to destroy some of Florida's rarest upland habitats. Although the local scrub and pine forests may already have been turned into pasture by the time Eaton arrived, thousands of acres of scrub elsewhere in the state were being plowed under to make way for the fruit.

This was because commercial growers had learned that high-quality citrus, if put on life support, could be grown on an industrial scale in the same high sandy places where scrub grew. The uplands were the only habitats in Florida where citrus could be grown because almost everywhere else was marsh. And as growers like to say, citrus doesn't like its feet to stay wet.

With the help of extra water and chemicals, Eaton Grove soon became one of the most celebrated in St. Petersburg. A 1921 photo shows luscious trees lining a boulevard near downtown—what is today Dr. Martin Luther King Jr. Street. When the trees were laden with blossoms or fruit, passersby must have seen a Garden of Eden. Photographs show a wagon stacked with crates of oranges, and another of pickers with sacks bulging with the fruit. In one 1922 photo, Mary's husband William clutches a fruit-laden branch, while she stands beside him proudly gripping an orange in her left hand as if lifting Earth itself.

In a way, she was.

About the time she planted her grove, the state's annual citrus production reached ten million boxes, and the alien orange had become the golden orb around which the state's economy had begun to orbit. With massive advertising in newspapers and magazines, Florida projected itself throughout the country as a paradise of low-hanging fruit. By 1909, Floridians had so fallen in love with this Asian orb that the state legislature voted the orange blossom the state flower.

The orange rose on the horizon of Florida's self-image like the sun it was often likened to. Although there was nothing remotely—let alone, uniquely—Floridian about the fruit, many people came to believe it indigenous. Truth is, orange groves covered millions of acres around the world, not only in the southeastern United States but through southeast Asia, southeastern Australia, parts of North American, central American, coastal regions of South America, in northern and southern Africa, and throughout the Mediterranean. Many varieties were considered superior to Florida's for certain uses.

As Florida endlessly catered to the orange, the state's real natural treasure—its desert gardens of scrub—was root-raked and replanted. Unlike the popular orange, scrub grew almost nowhere else. The scrub-jay lived nowhere else. Many of Florida's scrub-plants had evolved nowhere else. These treasures were being bartered away to make way for one of the world's most commonplace fruits. The endemic scrub-jay, once common in the middle-peninsula uplands, was declared threatened in 1987.

Advertisers imbued the golden ball of sunshine with myths of health and tropical vitality. The myth centered on the orange's supposedly natural presence in Florida. But the Florida scholar Scott D. Hussey wrote, " . . . the orange came to represent a 'natural' Florida through the conflation of the commercial product with the state's history by way of political and marketing puffery."

Early on, commercial groves began to disappear from highly populated urban areas like St. Petersburg even as they rapidly expanded throughout the upland countryside. In 1923, the land with Eaton's grove apparently became more valuable for building houses than for growing oranges. She sold her real estate to the developer John B. Green. Green used the magical aura to sell lots " . . . in one of the oldest and most beautiful orange groves in Pinellas county. The original trees have not been disturbed, except where necessary for the laying out of the streets and driveways. . . . You have always dreamed of a 'Florida Home Among the Oranges Blossoms.' Here is a golden opportunity to have your dreams come true." Trunk by trunk, orange trees fell, and houses grew—including the old American Foursquare our family would one day live in.

With commercial groves continuing to expand into scrub, by 1950 Florida was producing a hundred million boxes of citrus. In 1971, the harvest exceeded two hundred million boxes. This bounty was made possible by improved growing techniques. While feral orange varieties would grow in the woods, cultivating large quantities of commercial-grade oranges in Florida relied on what amounts to a crude form of hydroponic agriculture.

The impoverished sand gives the roots something to hold and keep the trees upright while growers saturate the substrate with water and fertilizer and, periodically, spray the trees with pesticides. In intensive care, citrus trees thrive in the warm, sunny greenhouse of Florida. But the image of oranges naturally rolling from the state's bosom is not so much a miracle of modern agriculture as a mirage of modern mythmaking. To make a go of it, growers had to marshal support of dozens of government laboratories, hundreds of scientists, and millions of public dollars for more than 120 years to support citrus in its struggle against diseases and pests that prey on a fruit ill-adapted to Florida.

In the late 1960s, the writer John McPhee described the extent of groves on the central ridge—much of it former scrubland—in his book *Oranges*: " . . . citrus trees cover it like a long streamer, sometimes as little as a mile and never more than twenty-five miles wide, running south, from Leesburg to Sebring, for roughly a hundred miles. It is the most intense concentration of citrus in the world."

Before citrus arrived, the central ridge held one of the most intense concentrations of Florida scrub-jays in the world.

By the late 1990s, scrub-jay populations had declined by as much as 90 percent as citrus growers turned thousands of acres of wild habitat into heavenly orange and grapefruit groves. Almost all the rarest, most ancient scrub was cleared on Lake Wales Ridge in the central peninsula, accelerating the scrub-jay's decline.

Citrus was not the only thing responsible for the decline of scrub. Ranchers cleared it for pasture, some that was later planted in groves. Other scrub was plowed under to make way for houses or industrial development. Phosphate mining destroyed thousands of acres of scrub. In many areas, the systematic suppression of fire, central to its ecology, caused scrub to become overgrown.

Between 1980 and the late 1990s, the land under citrus in southwest Florida alone—also once a stronghold of the scrub-jay—doubled to about 150,000 acres. By 2014, orange growers had turned almost 250,000 acres of southwest Florida into a water-guzzling, pesticide-laden paradise. According to Florida Citrus Mutual, a citrus growers' association, today nearly four thousand citrus growers statewide cultivate almost a half-million acres of land in Florida.

As of late, Florida's supposed tree of Eden has begun to shed some of its leaves because of new diseases. Many small growers have lost their family businesses. Packing plants have shut down. Faced with freezes and other obstacles, some growers have flipped their groves into housing developments, bought cheaper scrublands beyond the sprawl, and planted new groves.

Part of this is the result of unsustainable practices. Rather than eating a balanced diet as our parents taught us, the citrus industry gorged itself on a meal of oranges coming largely from a single stock. The incestuous gene pool of this monoculture invites large disease outbreaks because trees tend to suffer from the same genetic susceptibilities.

Most recently, the lethal citrus-greening disease has joined the centuries-old orange war. In the latest battle, this foreign pest—known in its native Asia as Huanglongbin—is attacking the non-native orange in a war waged between foreign adversaries on American soil.

With no clear end in sight to the devastation of citrus greening, the industry has fallen into a state of mourning. Magazine and newspaper articles lament the loss of jobs and a way of life. The suffering is real, the anguish palpable, the pain impossible to ignore. "Citrus Greening Threatens the Florida Economy and a Cherished Way of Life," reads a headline from *Sarasota Magazine*. From the *Tampa Bay Times* comes the news, "After almost 100 years, the last commercial grove in Tampa Bay in closing."

"A quarter of Florida's citrus acreage is gone," the 2018 article declares. "Twenty-five processing plants have become 12, and they're not operating at capacity. The state has lost $2 billion in economic impact . . . How sad it is to be an orange that isn't orange."

Hard enough on the big growers, citrus greening and other challenges have devastated mom-and-pop operations and some of the tens of thousands of people who worked in citrus or related industries. Especially hard hit have been migrant workers, whose futures were already uncertain enough. For others, the decline has brought deep nostalgia for a vanquished way of life.

The crisis facing citrus groves isn't nearly as bad as the crisis facing the scrub. Only fragments of the rarest scrub are left along Lake Wales Ridge, and the habitat is quickly vanishing in many other areas. The scrub-jay is being eliminated county by county and now occupies a tiny fraction of its former range.

If it is a time to mourn the orange, it is long past the time to mourn what citrus took away. With tens of millions of dollars and hundreds of scientists searching for a cure for citrus greening, the orange will survive in Florida. But with paltry funding for its cause and comparatively little political interest in its survival, the same cannot be said of the uniquely Florida bird and a habitat so rich in genuine Florida rarities.

When I step outside our house and see the ant excavations along the street, I imagine towering pines and scrub all around. I remember that while our home wasn't built *in* high pine, it was built *from* high pine. When we set out to replace some termite-eaten pine floorboards after buying the house, we were told the only longleaf heartwood to be found was from "sinker logs" salvaged from the bottom of rivers in north Florida where they had sunk on their way to sawmills more than a century ago. Where the tall pines used to sing in wind, now the old floorboards groan underfoot in the night.

Nostalgia is memory on a bender. It is to mourn the loss of orange groves without a thought for the original desert gardens citrus stole away. It is to mourn how citrus greening ate the heart out of the orange without a care for how the orange had long since eaten the heart out of the wild Florida scrub.

Seasons of Love

ERIKA HENDERSON

Many years ago, my father casually shared some of the best advice that I've ever heard. Our small family of three had recently moved to north central Florida from the southwest part of the state. Our new home had been built on land next to the place where his father and grandparents once lived. Wild plum, persimmon, and mayhaw trees surrounded remnants of the old homestead. According to my mother, I would follow my father track for track in those days. I certainly remember being shown the dog banana *Asimina reticulata* and warned about getting too close to the stinging nettle *Cnidoscolus stimulosus* or the prickly pear *Opuntia*.

These lessons in angry-plant identification were of particular importance in navigating the fields to sample the treats the land had to offer. The wild persimmons—frustratingly small at one to two inches in diameter with skin paper-thin, delicate, crispy, and sweet, similar to that of a date—were still delicious after the surprise of a stinging nettle encounter. But I would have to find and eat at least twice as many as usual of the bright-orange fruits in order to overcome the shock of the nettle. The same need for care applied when looking for wild blackberries and grapes—enjoy, appreciate, and eat the delicious treats from plants that could be found growing wild in the sandy soil all around, but watch out for the ones that could wreak havoc.

My father and I went on these walks often, and eventually I was able to differentiate between one small cluster of trees or healthy berry bushes over another. Ultimately, our trips would end with watering the newly planted fruit trees in the yard of our home. That great advice he gave me? As soon as you have built or bought your home, plant some fruit trees in the yard. Before you know it, you'll have delicious fruit to consume.

Over the years, we (mostly my father) planted muscadine grapes—some bronze, and others deep purple. Our gardens contained many "tests" of tomatoes, yellow, crookneck squash, cucumbers, and collard, mustard, and turnip greens. We grew small amounts of silver queen corn in the summertime along with peppers and melon. We tried apples (failed) and peaches (teeny tiny), and all the while, our citrus grew healthy and strong. Uncle Ed worked with my father on "tractoring" and planting techniques. Eventually, my father was growing Valencia peanuts and boiling them up with his secret technique to create the most delicious boiled peanuts this side of the Mississippi.

Beginning in the fall—right around Thanksgiving, to be exact—my father would begin the first round of taste tests. He would come inside the house after hours of working in the yard carrying a few choice selections from our citrus trees. Mind you, none of the pieces were ever fully ripe, but many were close, and that's where the excitement began. I would watch my father insert the blade of his pocketknife into the thin skin of a navel orange and deftly peel the fruit while creating a perfect spiral with the peel. He'd then slice the fruit near the top and, with a flick of his wrist, flip the top fifth back so I could with a gentle tug break the last intact membrane and separate the top from the rest of the fruit. Taking a bite of a peeled navel orange, feeling your teeth bite through the bright flavor of a fresh-picked piece of fruit and then chewing through the fibrous albedo or pith, is a treat to be experienced at least once. The juicy navel oranges with yellow and red centers he peeled and shared this way. Tangerine skin gave way easily, so my father handed them around, and we peeled them by hand. Tangelos and lemons he sliced in half and then quartered, and grapefruit he sliced in half and sprinkled with a touch of sugar.

My family would sample citrus until it was finally ready. Then, there were most marvelous juice blends—combinations of citrus to take advantage of each unique flavor. The perfectly round Hamlin orange gave sweet juice with little fiber because the pulp remained within the peel even after being squeezed in the citrus juicer. Next, the juice of a tangelo or two could be mixed in. Better yet, add some tangerine. Stir carefully, store in the fridge for an hour or more, and the result could outshine any commercial juice found in the grocery store. Citrus first begins to ripen in the winter, just in time for holiday gifts of fruit for friends and family. With trees steps away from the house, it was easy for my dad to make a carafe of fresh-squeezed orange juice for a morning meeting or event at work. Or to grab a pick-me-up tangerine for a friend or loved one. More than once I heard from friends who grew up in Florida and all over the country about the tradition of receiving the gift of a piece of citrus in their holiday stocking from their family.

The citrus season extended from winter through spring, followed by the smell of citrus blossoms in the late spring and the emergence of young fruit not long after. Each year, our yield increased. Some friends began to expect the annual treat, and others shared their own citrus in an effort to give back and to provide a basis for comparison. I learned of our pocket of protection: a combination of perfect tree placement near oak tree clusters and of being in an area where it just didn't get cold enough to kill the trees. That is, until it did. Some of our trees died back to the sour orange rootstock and returned with fruit so tart it could turn your mouth inside out. Other trees died completely from the freeze. This was true for many dooryard fruit enthusiasts, and devastating to the state citrus industry as a whole. The loss of the taste of a season gave perspective of a life without.

Before we proceed, let's take a look back. There is a Florida citrus story that I remember, and one I have only heard about. The version I remember is painted with thousands of citrus trees as far as the eye can see, lining the major roadways of the state. Depending on the time of year, one would see dots of brighter green or varying hues of orange in the perfectly coiffed uniform rows in the groves of citrus growers large and small. The trees were shaved on the sides (often with the aid of large machines) to allow for crews to do their best work. With ladders or simply an extended reach, these workers would pick a tree clean before moving on to the next. The fruit was then sent either to the packing house, the juice factory, or a roadside stand depending on the grade (quality) of that particular piece of fruit based on the standards set by the industries and largely the consumers supporting those industries. The Florida citrus story I recall involves stops at tourist attractions such as the Florida Citrus Tower and nearby establishments where one could try every citrus concoction ever created. I remember the burnt smell of orange juice being cooked/heat treated at juice plants and being taught that these factories let people all around the world taste Florida oranges.

The citrus story shared with me is more involved because it weaves more of the human element into this tale. Many people as far as north central Florida had at least one citrus tree in the yard (*as soon as you have built or bought your home . . .*). Regardless of bank account balance, it was easy to feel wealthy, even if just for a little while, with a few bushels of oranges on your very own tree. The ability to walk outside and pick a ripe orange or a tangerine from *your tree* and eat it right there, the burst of bright flavor at once satisfying both bodily thirst and hunger and other, loftier needs, the need for beauty, for nurturing, was a gift.

Need combined with opportunity drove many people, young and old, to travel far from their dooryards and their small communities in buses and other vehicles, all caravanning to areas of the state in need of workers to help with the citrus harvest, sometimes two to four hours away. Pickers came, too, from places such as Haiti, navigating a foreign region to contribute to our agricultural story. I often wonder what that experience was like. Being a young person of high school age, in college or beyond, gathering at a predetermined pickup spot with other people open to opportunity, riding in the dark for hours on end to a stranger's grove somewhere across the state. People of all races picked fruit. What was it like for them? In particular, what was that experience like for people of color before the civil rights era, and then at its peak?

The story shared doesn't focus on that particular view. Instead, a detailed picture of gorgeous citrus groves emerges, some of them the same groves I saw lining the highways while traveling through the center of the state. The citrus varieties grown were selected on the basis of reliability in flavor and desirability. A bountiful Hamlin or Valencia orange tree could produce hundreds if not thousands of glasses of citrus sunshine. And every viable piece of fruit needed to be picked. Soon, it was time to don a picking sack, a long, canvas bag with a wide opening and a strap along its length. A clip and hook found along the side of the opening at the top of the sack and again at the more narrow open bottom were linked in order to keep the contents inside until the sack was full and ready to be poured into a field box. When that time came, the picker detached the clip from the hook and guided the fruit from the sack into the field box, which held approximately ninety pounds of fruit. Pickers held contests among themselves: who had the best tree-selection skills, enabling them to find the tree with the best yield? How quickly could someone fill a box? (Important because payment was based on the number of boxes picked.) Who could find the most unusual-looking fruit? *This piece has a double navel, this one is colossally huge, this one has a bizarre shape . . .*

If you were a picker, you climbed ladders whenever necessary; you hauled bags of heavy fruit around on your back; you climbed, reached, descended, hoisted, poured. Suddenly, an orange represented so much more. A single object contained the very definition of work. Exhausting, but honest and dignified work.

Fast-forward a decade, plus a few years, and many of those citrus groves were razed due to either development or citrus canker, or both. The latter also affected homeowners, whose trees were destroyed by a state government in fear of losing the industry that employed so many. Enter another decade, and a series of freezes removed even more citrus. Proceed a bit further, and citrus greening threatens the future of citrus in the state like nothing that came before it.

Ducking beneath the dewy webs of large banana spiders suspended through the citrus trees, it is easy to get caught up in the beauty of a space. You are surrounded by pollinators and their sounds, some reverberating through the air, and others quieter. Shifts in the air create a gentle rustle of leaves. You tip up with your toe a seemingly perfect fruit lying on the ground and see that the downward-facing side is riddled with holes: evidence of birds attempting to find a snack. You examine the ground, discovering it is littered with fruit that is smaller than normal, disfigured, and a fade of colors from yellowish orange to green, as if one side of the fruit has been dipped in dye. A grove of sick and dying trees is disturbingly pretty. Even the bare limbs no longer able to produce citrus remain beautiful. These non-native trees have become a part of our Florida experience, and thus a part of our history. They have connected generations of family to one another, a daughter to her father, and Floridians to the land.

We appreciate the oranges: Parson Brown and Ambersweet, Pineapple, Hamlin, Temple, Page, sour, and of course the navel with flesh that is sweet, orange/red, or pink and a peel that is thin and able to be cut into a spiral. The tangelos: Nova, Orlando, and the embarrassingly juicy Mineola, aka the honeybell. The grapefruit: pink, white, and red, including the Duncan variety that was a star well before the *New York Times* gave it celebrity status. The lemons: Bearss, Ponderosa, and Meyer. The tiny fruits: kumquat and calamondin—oblong or round, sometimes sweet and sometimes . . . *not*. And finally, the tangerines: Dancy, sunburst, Murcott, and, worthy of its own bright, flashy sign—the Chinese honey: easy to peel, sweet, and likely to cause a mini-stampede at your local farmers' market with the ringing of the opening bell.

Biscayne National Monument

Preserving Our Precious Bays

NATHANIEL PRYOR REED

The world is filled with beautiful bays. They are hallmarks of almost every country that has access to the world's oceans. Some are surrounded by great cities, while others are highly productive estuaries that act as nurseries and fishing grounds

During the twentieth century, however, many of the world's bays were treated as refuse receptacles in hopes that dilution would handle the pollution. In response, many surrounding populations faced with dying bays fought for better environmental quality and tried to stop inappropriate development or industry.

One such battle occurred in the 1960s in beautiful Biscayne Bay, an aquamarine jewel southeast of Miami. Two proposed projects—the construction of a waterfront oil refinery and the development of barrier islands into a resort city to rival Miami Beach—set local conservationists into a flurry of action. Initially, it looked like a losing battle for bay lovers—after all, who would argue with projects that might boost jobs, tourism, and the local economy? But one group's brilliant arsenal of facts, publicity, and persistence, as well as a change in the political landscape, led to the 1968 creation of Biscayne National Monument, which later became a national park with the largest marine-scape—saved for future generations.

Biscayne Bay stretches thirty-five miles from Key Largo in the south to a northern lagoon between Miami and Miami Beach, the latter of which was damaged in the last century by sewage discharges, dredging, storm water, and agricultural runoff, and the creation and development of artificial and barrier islands. By the early twentieth century, a string of islands along the eastern part of the central bay was occupied by a handful of residents and farmers, with a few isles serving as weekend getaways for the wealthy. Disconnected from the mainland and with no utilities, these islands offered little opportunity for development, although they remained excellent hiding spots for pirates, wreckers, drug runners, and Caribbean refugees.

Improvements in technology and in human scheming, however, made the bay and its islands a target for development. One frequent proposal was to connect the islands to the mainland through a variety of causeway roads and bridges. Another included dredging the bay bottom to create artificial islands that would be home to high-rise hotels. This was the type of development that had created Miami Beach and was occurring throughout Florida—an effort to create waterfront property in a state that was booming with new residents who wanted watery access and beach views. Many of these proposals came and went until 1959 when Daniel K. Ludwig, an internationally known oil man of great wealth, bought 18,000 acres along the shore of Biscayne Bay. At first, he touted the property as a real estate development, but within two years the real plan became public: a port and industrial development near Homestead that included an oil refinery. The refinery would require a thirty-foot-deep channel across the bay and a forty-foot-deep port.

At the same time, plans for Islandia, a resort development on thirty barrier islands began to pick up steam. Some three hundred landowners, at the nod of Metro-Dade commissioners, incorporated Islandia into a city in 1961 despite a lack of roads, electricity, or infrastructure. However, Islandia now could issue municipal bonds to build the much-needed cause-way connection to the mainland that would make construction and tourism feasible. It also might end public access from the last undeveloped coast in the county.

Local government and business officials, along with area newspapers known for their boosterism, were thrilled at the projects' economic prospects. In 1962, Metro-Dade commissioners approved Ludwig's Seadade Realty, Inc., project (hereafter referred to as Seadade). A handful of dissenters, many of them members of the local Izaak Walton League, a prominent national conservation group, quickly joined ranks and created an organization to fight the proposals. They called themselves the Safe Progress Association (SPA) and, despite an initial budget of only $11.05, decided to take on the establishment.

SPA's leader was Lloyd Miller, a Pan American Airways employee in Miami and founder of the local Mangrove Chapter of the Izaak Walton League. Although other groups would join SPA in the Biscayne effort, in my opinion, Miller was the real leader of the battle. He was unstoppable. And before it finally ended, Miller's dog was poisoned, his car was damaged when he was shot at, and some people tried to get him fired from his job. But he never gave up, never wavered in his belief that the bay was too valuable to be sacrificed to the gods of industry.

Others working with Miller were author Polly Redford; her husband. Jim, who would go onto serve on the Metro-Dade commission; journalist Juanita Greene, whose persistence and writing slowly changed the stance of her employer, the *Miami Herald*; Belle Scheffel, who had great contacts with environmental and garden clubs; attorney Ed Corlett; and Lain Guthrie, an Eastern Airlines pilot. Guthrie had publicized the bay's problems with a very creative demonstration—he flushed orange-colored peanuts down the local power plant's toilets to prove (as they floated up) that the plant wasn't treating its sewage before dumping it into the bay. In support, SPA distributed a bumper sticker that featured a bright orange peanut and the slogan "NUTS to Dirty Industry."

SPA members spoke to any community group that would have them, arguing that the refinery project would bring air pollution and unavoidable oil spills into the bay—problems that would affect the quality of life and tourism. Dredging a deep-access channel would change the bay forever. Even a report by the Miami city manager about a refinery in Hawaii that showed large levels of "noxious pollutants" (and Seadade would be twice its size) didn't sway commissioners.

The economics had won over the Miami business community; Seadade promised to employ 18,540 people at an annual payroll of $130 million. That put SPA on a careful tightrope. Polly Redford best said it in 1964 when she wrote that SPA wasn't against industry, just that which was "dirty." With the associated infrastructure needed for a refinery, she warned: "Miamians, then, had reason to fear several square miles of stack industry on south bay just where prevailing winds and currents would spread its effluents over most of Dade County."

As the arguments dragged on and SPA attacked both projects from many angles, one idea took hold: seeking federal protection for the central and southern bay. It would halt development now and forever. And this is where I eventually got involved.

In the summer of 1962, several members of the community met with Miller to discuss how to save the bay and its islands. The state and county, as Miller recalled, seem to have no interest in this angle, so "we wondered if we could interest the federal government." The next day, Miller called Joe Penfold, national conservation director for the Izaak Walton League, and told him about the unfolding situation. Penfold said the only permanent win for the bay might be federal protection—perhaps as a national monument or a national park. Using his contacts, Penfold got the idea to U.S. Secretary of the Interior Stewart Udall, who sent a department team to study the environmental features of the bay. At the same time, Udall sent a letter to Secretary of the Army Cyrus Vance asking that the Seadade permit be withheld until the federal government could be assured that the nearby Everglades National Park (which came under Udall's authority and protection) and the John Pennekamp Coral Reef Preserve (now a state park) wouldn't be damaged by refinery pollution.

What the team found was astounding. Even local residents and SPA members didn't realize the value of the bay's biodiverse natural resources. The bay was home to the northern portion of the Florida coral reef; "luxuriant turtle grass beds;" tropical hardwood trees on the islands; and a treasure trove of wildlife. Udall's team decided the biota was of "national significance" and deserved protection.

During a November 1963 visit to the area, Udall confirmed his support for designating the area a national monument—at the time, it was too small to be a national park. When Polly Redford asked Udall for advice about how and if conservation groups should keep up the battle against industrial and agricultural interests, Udall replied: "We are losing the battle to keep America beautiful. You must band together more to make a stronger fight for conservation. It is not cheap, it's not easy but I say to you—persist, work hard, work together."

The gears quickly went in motion to put together a national monument. Although the president can use the 1906 Antiquities Act to designate federal lands as national monuments, that would not be the case in Biscayne. The monument would include islands in private ownership—including the mythical Islandia project that would have to be federally purchased—so Congress had to approve and fund it. U.S. Rep. Dante Fascell, who represented the Biscayne area, became its tireless promoter, repeatedly introducing legislation, beginning in 1966, to make it a reality. Another great supporter was Herbert Hoover Jr. of the same-named vacuum company, who pledged $100,000 toward island purchases if the monument was approved.

Islandia owners tried many methods to thwart preservation, including efforts to construct a four-lane causeway highway to and through the islands, even a toll road, knowing full well that Udall considered such work incompatible with a national monument. Miller fought the project, noting that the work "would destroy 50 percent of the marine biology and choke off 200 square miles of bay bottom." Thankfully, the causeways never were approved.

Another player in the project was the state of Florida, which held title to the bay bottom and would have to transfer 92,000 acres of it to the federal government for a monument. During his 1966 campaign, Florida Governor Claude Kirk opposed Biscayne protection, siding with corporate interests who viewed it as a federal landgrab. However, Kirk was an interesting character whose mind could be swayed when confronted with strong facts. And I was his new environmental advisor.

In this case, a trip into the bay made all the difference.

I loved the bay—still do. My wife Alita and I have spent many wonderful hours there fishing, especially for large bonefish that swim in its sparkling waters. I was friends with many guides and a Florida Marine Patrol officer that worked in the Keys. That contact would prove invaluable.

After the election ended, Kirk told me that he planned to take a multiday sailboat cruise on Biscayne Bay with the lovely "Madame X," whom he later married. (Her real name was Erika Mattfeld, but Kirk told the press her name was Madame X, and they ate it up.) At the time, I said, "Governor, are you really capable of sailing a 38-foot boat alone?" I pointed out the area's treacherous tides, shoals, and reefs that could be troublesome. When he admitted that he might need some help, I set him up with my Marine Patrol friend. I advised the officer that at some point "you're going to find time to explain to the governor how uniquely beautiful the islands are and how incredibly productive the bay is; both within minutes of a major city." I had told Kirk about the issues in the bay, particularly the island development scheme, which I called "the mythical land of Islandia," hoping to get him to change his mind on the issue. He liked to see things in black and white, in good versus evil, so I tried to frame the Islandia controversy in this way.

As expected, the governor and his lady friend became bored after a couple of days and managed to run the boat hard aground as they tried to navigate Card Sound. There was nothing to do but wait for three hours for the tide to rise; Madame X went below deck, and Kirk drank beer with the officer, who took the opportunity to talk about the bay's beauty and wildlife and the threats that would come from dredges, causeways, and refineries. The governor came to believe that an evil empire was behind the potential destruction of this chain of pearls. When he came back on land, he accused me of setting it all up. I laughed . . . and then we launched a state/federal effort to protect the bay. This effort included the state denying any permits for causeways or dredging—the very things that Islandia developers needed. Kirk's change of heart was critical, and now Islandia was sunk. He was completely on board with saving the bay, wondering, "How could those greedy so-and-so's want to create another Miami Beach? They don't realize they will destroy one of the most beautiful bays in the world. Let's get going and save Biscayne Bay!"

A change in local government also ensured the death of Seadade and Islandia. Two bay preservers were elected in 1964 to the Metro-Dade Commission, whose approval was necessary for various issues, including a building permit for Ludwig and Seadade. That same year Seadade withdrew its refinery plans, instead proposing an industrial seaport for the waterfront site in the southern bay. A year later, the commission decided to support the national monument project and oppose any causeway; Udall had warned that a causeway or similar access would end national monument consideration.

It was a new environmental era in Miami. Even the angry landowners on Elliott Key, which would have been central to the Islandia development, couldn't stop it. They plowed a one-hundred-foot-wide, seven-mile-long road down the middle of the island, destroying much of its flora, in hopes that it would no longer be desirable for protection. They were wrong and today that road, known as "Spite Highway," is slowing filling back in with native vegetation.

I'm proud to say that on October 18, 1968, Congress approved Biscayne National Monument. President Lyndon B. Johnson, who had fished in the bay, signed it into law that same day. The new monument preserved 96,300 acres, and its enacting legislation stated that it was created "in order to preserve and protect for the education, inspiration, recreation and enjoyment of present and future generations a rare combination of terrestrial, marine, and amphibious life in a tropical setting of great natural beauty . . ."

The first person to sell property for the new monument was Lancelot Jones, a well-known fishing guide who grew up on Porgy Key. His father, an ex-slave, had raised a family and farmed on three barrier islands, growing limes, vegetables and pineapples, as many people in the area did in those days. Although many of his neighbors hoped to get rich by developing the keys into Islandia, Jones spurned the idea and endorsed bay preservation.

I once asked Jones whether the potential of vast income was worth sacrificing his beloved tract of land.

He quietly replied, "No, I thought so months ago, but wanted a land-to-sea legacy for others to enjoy."

Jones received a life estate in the land deal so he could enjoy the rest of his years on Porgy Key; he stopped living there after Hurricane Andrew destroyed all its structures in 1992. Jones died five years later at age ninety-nine. Since 2013 the Jones Family Historic District has been listed on the National Register of Historic Places.

There have been two expansions of the monument, and in 1980 Congress declared it to be Biscayne National Park. Today, the park is a unique gem in the National Park Service. It is the largest marine park in the country, with 95 percent of its 173,000 acres underwater. More than half a million people each year visit to enjoy its beauty and recreational opportunities, including fishing, snorkeling, kayaking, and diving.

It has many threats, mostly owing to its proximity to the booming Miami metropolitan area. But thanks to Lloyd Miller, SPA, and indefatigable bay advocates, today there is no refinery, no channel, and no Islandia high-rise resort. It is where endangered manatees, bonefish, tarpon, and butterflies exist in subtropical wonder.

Biscayne Bay is a place where many generations to come will be able to see the raw splendor of Florida's precious Biscayne Bay. Perhaps they can look out at it as I have and be awed by a sunrise, and hook a bonefish or tarpon, and enjoy a day of peace on the water.

It is my hope for Florida's future.

PART VI

AT THE HEART

Some Days the Sea

RICHARD BLANCO

The sea is never the same twice. Today
the waves open their lions-mouths hungry
for the shore and I feel the earth helpless.
Some days their foamy edges are lace
at my feet, the sea a sheet of green silk.
Sometimes the shore brings souvenirs
from a storm, I sift spoils of sea grass:
find a broken finger of coral, a torn fan,
examine a sponge's hollow throat, watch
a man-of-war die a sapphire in the sand.
Some days there's nothing but sand
quiet as snow, I walk, eyes on the wind
sometimes laden with silver-tasting salt,
sometimes still as the sun. Some days
the sun is a dollop of honey and raining
light on the sea-glinting diamond dust,
sometimes there are only clouds, clouds—
sometimes solid as continents drifting
across the sky, other times wispy, white
roses that swirl into tigers, into cathedrals,
into hands, and I remember some days

I'm still a boy on this beach, wanting
to catch a seagull, cup a tiny silver fish,
build a perfect sand castle. Some days I am
a teenager blind to death even as I watch
waves seep into nothingness. Most days
I'm a man tired of being a man, sleeping
in the care of dusk's slanted light, or a man
scared of being a man, seeing *some* god
in the moonlight streaming over the sea.
Some days I imagine myself walking
this shore with feet as worn as driftwood,
old and afraid of my body. Someday,
I suppose I'll return *someplace* like waves
trickling through the sand, back to sea
without any memory of being, but if
I could choose eternity, it would be here
aging with the moon, enduring in the space
between every grain of sand, in the cusp
of every wave, and every seashell's hollow.

From *A Seminole Legend*

The Life of Betty Mae Tiger Jumper

BETTY MAE TIGER JUMPER AND PATSY WEST

I remember the days when I used to see the old people sit around the camp-fires. The campfire consisted of large logs and four dead oak logs burning in the middle. That was where all women cooked the family's meals. Early in the morning before the sun rose, the older men started the fires so the ladies could cook. The men usually put on the coffee first, and they drank it while the meal was being cooked.

At noontime most of the men were out either hunting or working, so the women and kids ate leftovers such as meat, bread, biscuits, and coffee. The evening meal was eaten before the sun went down.

Children between five and seven years of age were taught to fetch water, sofki, and coffee for guests and to ask them to sit down. A child's first task was to learn how to cook.

The main food was swamp cabbage. The cabbage palm was chopped down in order to get the heart of the palm. It was brought back to camp, put in a big pot with a small amount of water, covered, and simmered for an hour or so. Honey and pork grease were added for flavor.

Many Indians were scared to eat turkey, thinking its spirit was bad and it would make you sick. Some Indians who do eat turkey will get the medicine man to doctor over the turkey before it's ready to cook and eat. That would as-sure that they wouldn't get sick from eating it.

Many Seminoles survived on garfish, for there were many in canals and ponds. The fish can keep for days if it is hung in a chickee.

Water turtles were also meat for Indians. Turtles were roasted by a campfire—turned until they were cooked. Then they were broken open, and the meat was spread on palm leaves. Some turtles were put in soup. The land turtles, called gophers, have to be dug out of a deep hole that they dig in the sand. The gopher has a better taste than water turtles.

Alligator meat was also eaten by the Seminoles. They would slice on the side of the tail to get the best part. Seminoles also took their hides and sold them to the white people.

When the men went hunting for honey, they would carry with them an ax, matches, and a net to cover themselves with. When they found a tree with a honeybees' nest, they would build a fire in the direction where they wanted the tree to fall. They would then chop the tree down. After it fell, a man would cover himself and smoke the bees out of the hive. He got all of the honey, put it in a bucket, and took it back to the camp. Honey was used to sweeten cornbread, lemonade, and sour oranges. The women sometimes cooked taffy for the kids to pull apart and eat. Honey was the only sweetener.

Corn sofki is made out of dry corn. Women pound the corn in a hole carved out of a stump. Then the large kernels are cooked to make sofki, and the finely ground corn is used for grits and cornmeal. Sofki is cooked with water in a big pot. Certain tree roots, called cappie, were burned, and the ashes were mixed with water to flavor the sofki.

After the evening meal, children gathered around the campfire for the older people to tell them stories. That was the way that the young people were taught the rules of life and their clan's ways. Those rules were to be followed. . . .

During my early childhood I had a lonely life. It seemed that my closest friends were my dogs and cats, and a bunny that a white couple gave me. I taught them to get along with each other, which amazed the reservation visitors who stopped by our camp. I could easily relate to my grandmother's stories about talking animals, such as the mischievous rabbit. Nights under the mosquito net in my grandmother's chickee and days in the field picking tomatoes also gave me plenty of time to hear the oral history and legends of our tribe and clan. The old folks used to say:

- When you hear a red bird sing near you, it's a sign you're going to have a visitor from far away.

- Never put a ring on her pointing finger or thumbs—they'll never bend again.
- If a bear is killed to eat, when it is cooked never put salt on it. It is believed that if you do, when you go into the woods, it will kill you.
- If you are out in the Everglades and hear a woman cry at a distance, don't answer or try to go out to see what the problem is, because the cry is a panther, trying to lure you out to kill you.
- When there are lots of mosquitoes, a fire is built in the yard near camp and also under chickees. Lots of leaves are thrown on the fires to make smoke and drive the mosquitoes away.
- Don't ever wear feathers of birds around your head or carry them, because your neck will turn and you can't get it straight again, until the medicine man puts medicine on it.
- Bear's claws or bones cannot be worn unless first doctored by the medicine man.
- Books belong to white peoples—not Indians—and you never look at them.
- When a baby was swinging in his or her swing, a little medicine bundle must be tied on the swing to keep away the evil spirits.
- Young people should never stare at older people or look at them or stand near them.
- When there's a strong rain and heavy thunder and lightning, don't move around—just sit still, or you might see a cut hand with a painted thumb under the table where you are sitting.

It was summer and hurricane season, which brought the worst weather that we Seminoles ever experienced. Grandpa Jimmie Gopher was in charge of preparing for the storm. Even though he was a Christian, he knew that our Indian medicine had to be made to combat these fierce storms.

The number four is important in Indian culture and medicine. You always do things in four. Like, if you take medicine, you take four sips. You always have four logs in the fire.

The first thing Grandpa did was to get four axes. One he got from the woodpile where he cut the wood. I don't know where he got the other three, but he got them. He jammed the handles into the ground so the blades were facing out in the direction that the wind would be coming. This, he said, would slow and turn the big wind away.

After he put the axes in the ground, he jumped up and went around whooping and yelling four times. This was a powerful chant to protect us. He also made a fire and blew smoke against the wind.

[When we lived in Indiantown], I remember, the chickees were built so that the roofs could slide down on the corner poles and lie flat on the ground. When Indians knew the big wind [ho-tale-tha-ko] was coming, they would drop the chickee roof to the ground. Then the entire family would crawl under the roof and stay there until the storm passed. In all the years I have known, no Indian ever lost a life while being sheltered under a chickee roof.

My family always seemed to know if the big wind was going to be strong or light. One time my mother said to me when I was about ten years old, "follow me," and I did.

She said, "you know the big wind is coming." I said I had heard the adults talking about it. She said she would tell me how to tell if the storm would be bad.

She pointed to the dark sky where the storm seemed to be coming from and she said, "we will stand here and you will know how strong the wind is going to be."

I stood with my mother a while and finally she pointed toward a bird way up in the sky. She said, "You see that bird high in the sky?" I said, "yes." She said, "Well, that bird with the fork tail [the Man-o-War bird] is the one that will tell you how strong the wind is going to be."

"If that bird is flying low it means the wind will be real strong. When the bird is high, like this one, it means the wind isn't going to be strong."

She was right. That storm wasn't bad. She said this was how our people lived through the big winds. By looking at that bird, they knew if the winds would be strong or not.

. . .

At times my memory goes back to the days when I used to see old people sit around a campfire. After the evening meal is over, children gather around for older people to tell them stories. This was the way that young people were taught the rules of life and their clan's ways. I am glad to say that this helped me to live and learn, and to abide by the outside world's rules and laws as well.

Before we learned how to work within the system, people liked to see us wrestle alligators, make patchwork, operate a few stores, and work in commercial tourist villages where people pay to go see Indians. As long as we were there, people liked to see us. But we learned how to fight for our rights the same as anyone else.

Some people still like to see us as we were back in the 1920s or 1930s. But many young people are interested in a higher standard of living, as in the outside world. The money we make from cigarettes and bingo goes into tribal improvements so in the future our younger generation doesn't have to sit by roads trying to sell little baskets or dolls.

A Plea for Wider Justice

MARJORY STONEMAN DOUGLAS

Miami Herald, January 3, 1921

The little wiggly single worm
When trodden on ungently
Can be depended on to turn
(A poor rhyme, incidentally)
But what I mean is just that he
Is similar to you and me.

An oyster, bivalve, placid, calm,
Will get quite vexed by grit,
Protecting its fat self from harm
By coating over it.
It makes a pearl of white smooth beauty
Nor ever prates of "art" or "duty."

The jelly fish when prodded shrinks
As you and I do.
Thus proving that who thinks he thinks
May know a thing or two.
But this I state, for his correction.
He always acts for his protection.

So let's extend democracy
To fit these things inferior,
Who really aren't, because you see
We're not darned superior.
We only like to think we are.
But they aren't so particular.

Florida Is a Pretty Girl

FRANCES SUSANNA NEVILL

If pretty were a degree, my mama would have a PhD. She was, and still is, at 73, bona fide pretty. She has all the regalia to prove it: the coveted crowns, scepters, and trophies. Old photos (some that made the local paper) show her seated on a throne laden with sprays of roses and tropical Florida blooms. A small town "pretty girl," she mesmerized crowds of onlookers at county fairs with her then-considered "exotic" Greek American looks—alluring ebony eyes, lustrous raven-dark hair, olive skin tanned just a bit more by her childhood and teenage years banking time on Clearwater Beach. The judges frequently gave her the crown even though she was, by far, the tiniest girl, the underdog. "I have a tall personality," she would say throughout my childhood.

Truth is, my entire hometown in rural Central Florida was filled with "pretty." Dense with rolling hills and citrus trees, it was also home to a lot of good-looking women. Even today, I can think of a dozen wholesomely beautiful women— homecoming queens, pageant girls, rodeo girls, girls who worked at the bank, girls who worked in the grocery store, girls who worked in the groves, girls who worked in the fields. Florida postcards by the hundreds if not thousands featured local beauties exposing gleaming smiles like sunflowers. Underwater mermaids at Weeki Wachee, water skiers at Cypress Gardens, beach bunnies frolicking along the sand remain enduring symbols linking Florida to beauty.

My grandfather, back when I was a young girl, thought one woman he met while running a small grocery store in one of the poorest parts of town, was "too pretty" to be struggling. He thought she should be in a professional job.

He even helped her get one. He didn't make a pass at her; he wanted nothing in return. He wasn't trying to be a do-gooder. He just thought she was pretty and knew she was smart, too, so he employed his local power to give her a leg up. No doubt, her prettiness is what first grabbed him, though. Just being honest. Don't e-mail me or Twitter me over this. Don't get all up in arms. You react to beauty, too. And this is my point. Pretty can sure cast a spell.

I've seen the ugly side of pretty, too. When my parents divorced and my mother, never educated beyond high school, was left adrift with two young daughters, no money, no prospects, no visions or dreams for herself, I saw her prettiness taken advantage of. Lustful men wandered in and out of whatever house we were living in, in and out of her life, in and out of mine. Not that she was an innocent victim. She understood the currency of pretty and traded it for what she needed to get by.

Florida is a pretty girl, too. Probably the prettiest in the room. I've walked many of her beaches along her peninsula that dangles out into two seas—the Gulf and the Atlantic. On a January 2020 evening, I meander along a strip of beach (I'll keep my favorite spot to myself even though developers have already gotten their hands on it) that is no less mesmerizing than it was in my youth. The Gulf waters, mason-jar blue, roll up on slick wet sand that's speckled with shards of pastel shells. The rush of foam-capped water bubbles white like meringue at your feet. Cars and boats dump thousands of visitors daily that crowd along the powdery quartz carpet that outlines this state, but for me it is a place for enjoyable solitude. The elixir of salt air produces a dreamlike effect I find more intoxicating than any drink or drug. People who pay attention find *who they are* in those moments, on these same walks along the strand. There is a peace in meeting up with yourself in these places, and often an awakening. These encounters in life aren't easy to just conjure up. Like hunting for sea glass or pristine sand dollars, you have to work toward finding them. Even for a local, like myself, it takes time and prioritization to meet up with nature. And like beauty, they should be appreciated and not sullied.

Our many visitors and residents endure the misery of—well, I'll say it—the North and escape to Florida. Florida can't be found in Ohio, Indiana, or New Jersey. It can't be found in leafless birch trees, dour gray skies pregnant with post-Christmas snow and stinging, biting, frigid, pissing rains. Florida rains are glorious explosions of force; torrents of water accompanied by lightning bolts that shatter the sky. Heat lightning in the summer marbles the sky with shades of fuchsia and lavender clouds. Storms pass quickly here, unlike the weeks and months of lingering gray skies and snowstorms in other places.

As a fourth-generation Floridian, I can't help but feel anger at what has been done to this beautiful place. I think about what has been done to her for decades of people having their way with her. As with my mother, charming people bring their sweet talk, take what they want, and wander off to other green pastures without a moment's thought. Along Florida's shore, she's about run out of room for all of the pavement and construction that line her arms like the needle tracks of a heroin addict. Growth built on crushing nature is a kind of addictive drug here. You can trace on a map the Florida Wildlife Corridor, which aims to link wild areas that will help maintain the state's biodiversity. I wonder how panthers and black bears follow a map they cannot comprehend. We've squeezed them so far down the state and crammed them so far inland, I'm thinking they'll only be able to hang out along a turnpike rest stop.

Appalachian literature is filled with stories of how coal extraction and mountaintop removal devastates the landscapes and demoralizes its people. Florida knows a thing or two about this. Her interior spaces have been explored, drilled, plunged, and mined to their deepest, darkest depths. Our pristine springs are deleted by bottling companies sucking out our lifeblood. Lagoons and waterways with rich fish populations that sustain many people and draw tourists the world over are poisoned by brown runoff water filled with fertilizer, gasoline, and other poisons. And she can't stop them. No one seems to be watching as "progress" drives on like a piston. The state's beauty lures in the chancers, users, gamblers, and speculators who leave her sullied.

Decades ago, pawing onlookers wanted to not only take her youthful beauty, they wanted to cut her in half like the hapless magician's assistant who is put into a box while the magician rips down through her abdomen with the sharp blade of a saw. But with that scenario, we all know, it's an illusion. The pretty assistant with the corset top and fishnet hose and tendrils of brown locks will jump out and say, "ta da." Trick over. With Florida, what they wanted to do was real. They actually proposed butchering her up and splitting her wide open in some hackneyed scheme they called the Cross Florida Barge Canal. Thankfully, she had a de facto fairy godmother in the room—Marjorie Harris Carr, to be specific—to stand up and protect her.

It's April 2020. I rang in the New Year like everyone else and never thought a global pandemic was brewing amidst all of the "new year, new me" optimism that was sweeping the world (what in God's hell was I thinking when I posted "#2020isgoingtobemyyear" on Instagram?). Winter and spring in Florida, for me, are usually filled with hikes through hammocks and long walks on the beaches. Those places are all now closed due to the COVID-19 virus. While the virus is ruthlessly snaking its way like the thousands of invasive pythons in the Everglades, across the globe stealing lives, overrunning hospitals and health care workers, devastating economies, and depressing the spirit of so many people, I am also reading anecdotes that the water along Florida's shores has never been more clear. I am reading about rare sightings of sea turtles and the endangered small-tooth sawfish seen swimming in South Florida. While I know that man's return to nature is imminent—the waterways will indeed re-open, the beaches will once again be crowded with tourists and locals alike, the trails will be packed with hikers hungry for exploration—I wonder if once people are confronted with Florida's inherent beauty and her wildness that brings about a restorative peace, will they honor her? Will they show her gratitude for being there waiting for them looking, apparently, prettier than she has in a long time; healthier than she has in a long time? Will they honor her for being the giver she is? Or will they just continue to take?

I know what happened to my mother. Yes, her eyes still have a glimmer and a sparkle. Genetics have trumped the imprint a life of struggle and hardship did to her spirit. My mother had the ability to decide where and when she would allow her beauty to be manhandled and taken for free. But what can I say for Florida? Before the pandemic: Florida was plagued with human-induced algae blooms swamping her shores; piping hot pavement covering her surface with a never-ending series of road projects; water siphoned and hauled off in trucks; minerals mined, trees butchered, pesticides strangling the scent of orange blossoms. Oh, and that distinct scent of orange blossoms might just be something remembered by old-timers in just a few decades.

One has to ask: where are her parents? In an era when helicopter moms and dads buzz about every playground and school, where are Florida's parents? She should be showered with bouquets and celebrated and loved. "Florida" literally means "land of flowers." She should flourish and blossom, and if a crown could be placed on her head, we should all line up to give her one. Look at what she has given and continues to give us. Unlike my mother, she can't make decisions for herself. She can't tell them to "stop" or say "no means no." She can't tell them that she needs more from them than what they are taking. She can't tell them that what they are doing in the name of "enjoyment" or "pleasure" is coming at too high of a cost to her survival. She can't voice her pain in a language they seem to understand. She can't even say "that hurts."

I mean, how much more can a girl take?

Acknowledgments

The authors are indebted to the "anonymous" readers of the original manuscript, Janine Farver, Jeff Klinkenberg, and Craig Pittman, for suggestions that enriched this collection. We also thank Meredith Babb of the University of Florida Press for inviting us to work on this wonderful project and John Wentworth for his editing work on *The Wilder Heart*. We are grateful to the family of Nathaniel Pryor Reed, especially his son Adrian, for permission to use Reed's essay in this volume; it originally was published in *Travels on the Green Highway: An Environmentalist's Journey*. Many thanks as well to Jeff Ripple and Susan Cerulean, editors of *The Wild Heart of Florida*, the book that served as the foundation for this one, and for their leadership in preserving and protecting Florida's natural treasures—which make a better place for all.

Contributors

ANMARI ALVAREZ-ALEMÁN is the Caribbean Research Director at the Clearwater Marine Aquarium. She received a bachelor's degree in biology and master's degree in integrated management of coastal zones from the University of Havana, Cuba, and a PhD in interdisciplinary ecology from the University of Florida. Her work focuses on gathering scientific information that contributes to the local and regional conservation of the West Indian manatee.

LARS ANDERSEN is author of *Paynes Prairie, The Great Savanna: A History and Guide*, and a full-time river guide for Adventure Outpost. He and his wife Patsy live in the Ichetucknee forest near Ft. White, Florida.

CYNTHIA BARNETT is an award-winning environmental writer working on her fourth book, a story of seashells and the animals that build them. She is a fifth-generation Floridian raising a sixth generation in Gainesville, where she is also environmental journalist in residence at the University of Florida.

RICHARD BLANCO, conceived in Cuba, born in Spain, and raised in the United States, is a poet, public speaker, author, and civil engineer who served as the inaugural poet at President Barack Obama's second inauguration. His poetry has appeared in several literary journals, and he is the author of six books.

LOREN G. "TOTCH" BROWN (1920–1996) was a multigeneration native of Chokoloskee who spent most of his life in the Everglades as a commercial fisherman, alligator hunter, and writer. He won a Bronze Star during World War II at the Battle of the Bulge.

GABBIE BUENDIA is an educator working for a future where environmental experiences are just and inclusive. In her free time, she enjoys cooking and going to dance class.

BUFFALO TIGER was born in the Everglades in 1920 and served as the first elected tribal chairman of the Miccosukee Nation, assuming office in 1962, the year the Miccosukee gained federal recognition.

RICK CAMPBELL is a poet and essayist living on Alligator Point, Florida. His latest collection of poems is *Gunshot, Peacock, Dog*. He has published five other poetry books as well as poems and essays in numerous journals, including *The Georgia Review*, *Fourth River*, *Kestrel*, and *New Madrid*. He has won a Pushcart Prize and a National Endowment for the Arts Fellowship in Poetry. He teaches in the Sierra Nevada College MFA program.

FREDERICK R. DAVIS is head of and professor in the Department of History at Purdue University. He also holds the R. Mark Lubbers Chair in the History of Science. His most recent book is *Banned: A History of Pesticides and the Science of Toxicology*. A lifelong birder, he studied the history of science at Harvard, the University of Florida, and Yale, where he received his PhD.

JACK E. DAVIS, University of Florida professor of history and Rothman Family Chair in the Humanities, is the author of *The Gulf: The Making of an American Sea*, winner of the 2018 Pulitzer Prize in history. In 2019 he was awarded an Andrew Carnegie Fellowship to support his current book project, "Bird of Paradox: How the Bald Eagle Saved the Soul of America."

MARJORY STONEMAN DOUGLAS (1890–1998) is best known for her 1947 classic *The Everglades: River of Grass* and as the voice of Everglades protection. She was the author of several nonfiction and fiction books. Born in Minnesota, she lived in South Florida from 1915 until her death at the age of 108.

ISAAC EGER spent most of his early life escaping Florida. Now he's back to see his birthright to its end. You can find his work in the publications that will tolerate him.

LAUREN GROFF is the author of five books, most recently the novel *Fates and Furies* and the story collection *Florida*, both finalists for the National Book

Award. She has been a Guggenheim and Radcliffe fellow, and her work has been published in over thirty languages. She lives in Gainesville, Florida.

CLAY HENDERSON, an environmental lawyer formerly with Holland & Knight, has served on the Volusia County Council, Florida Constitution Revision Commission, Indian River Lagoon National Estuary Program Policy Committee, Indian River Lagoon Management Conference, and as director of Stetson University Water Institute and president of Florida Audubon Society. He has received lifetime-achievement awards from the Marine Resources Council and the Environmental and Land Use Section of the Florida Bar, and a national public service award from The Nature Conservancy.

ERIKA HENDERSON received life lessons disguised as food-growing tips from her father, who inspired her to grow, maintain, harvest, and sell citrus at a local farmers' market until citrus greening entered the north central portion of the state of Florida. Erika named her venture Henderson and Daughter Plants and Produce and appreciates the support of her loving parent.

LEE IRBY teaches Florida history at Eckerd College and has written about the state's environment and culture for twenty years. He is the author of three novels, a slew of short fiction, and a smattering of plays. He appeared in the film *Spring Breakers* as the History Professor.

BETTY MAE TIGER JUMPER (1923–2011) was the first female chief of the Seminole Tribe of Florida and founder of its first newspaper, *The Seminole News*. A long-time newspaper editor and author or coauthor of three books, she received the first lifetime achievement award from the Native American Journalism Association.

HARRY A. KERSEY JR. is professor emeritus in history at Florida Atlantic University and the author of several books, including *An Assumption of Sovereignty: Social and Political Transformation among the Florida Seminoles*.

RUSS KESLER is a native Floridian. He is retired from teaching writing at the University of Central Florida. His books of poetry are *A Small Fire* and *As If*.

CHARLES LEE is director of advocacy for Audubon Florida and manages Florida Audubon Society's wildlife sanctuaries. During his forty-seven years on the staff of the Florida and National Audubon societies, he helped establish Florida's first wetlands protection and environmental land-acquisition programs. Gubernatorial appointments to numerous panels and commissions have included service on the Commission on the Future of Florida's Environment, which led to the creation of Preservation 2000 and its successor, Florida Forever, premier state land acquisition programs.

SUSAN LILLEY is a Florida native and inaugural Poet Laureate of Orlando. Her poetry and essays have appeared in *American Poetry Review, Gulf Coast, The Southern Review,* and other journals. Her collection *Venus in Retrograde* was published in April 2019.

DAVID MCCALLY, born and raised in Pensacola, has an intimate knowledge of Florida, having earned degrees from three of the state's universities and taught at four, developing special expertise in environmental and African American histories along the way. He currently resides in Gainesville, at long last in peace.

BILL MAXWELL, a native of Fort Lauderdale, is an award-winning syndicated columnist and editorial writer who joined the *St. Petersburg Times* (now *Tampa Bay Times*) in 1994. He has taught English and journalism at the college level for two decades, and in 2013 was writer in residence at Everglades National Park.

LUCINDA FAULKNER MERRITT has a history with Florida's springs that dates back to the 1950s. As the communications coordinator with the Ichetucknee Alliance and blogger at http://awordwitch.blogspot.com, her central message is that we are all connected to the Floridan aquifer, to the springs, and to each other. She lives near Rum Island with her life partner, Forrest, and several cats.

FRANCES SUSANNA NEVILL is a writer, professor, and advocate. She helped advance policy and awareness for conservation in both the Florida Legislature and working for The Nature Conservancy's Florida Chapter. She has an MFA in fiction and her work appears in magazines and journals. Frances lives in Orlando with her two daughters and is working on her first novel and short story collection.

LESLIE KEMP POOLE is a fourth-generation Floridian with a love of small towns, country backroads, wildflower fields, and blackwater rivers. She is assistant professor of environmental studies at Rollins College and author of *Sav-*

ing Florida: Women's Fight for the Environment in the Twentieth Century, which focuses on the little-told role of women in saving the state's natural resources.

NATHANIEL "NAT" PRYOR REED (1933–2018) was a tireless champion for Florida's environment, having worked through governmental agencies and then as a volunteer to protect natural areas, especially the Everglades. Reed began his career as an advisor to Florida Governor Claude Kirk and went on to serve as U.S. Assistant Secretary of the Interior during the Nixon and Ford administrations, where he championed the creation of Biscayne National Monument. His essay in this collection previously was published in his 2016 autobiography *Travels on the Green Highway: An Environmentalist's Journey.*

GIANNA RUSSO is the author of the poetry collections *One House Down* and *Moonflower,* winner of a Florida Book Award, and two chapbooks, *Blue Slumber* and *The Companion of Joy.* She is assistant professor of English and creative writing at Saint Leo University, where she teaches in both the undergraduate and graduate programs and serves as editor-in-chief of *Sandhill Review* and as director of the Sandhill Writers Retreat.

BRUCE STEPHENSON is an environmental studies professor at Rollins College and directs the ecological restoration of the Genius Preserve for the Elizabeth Morse Genius Foundation. The author of the award-winning *John Nolen: Landscape Architect and City Planner,* he enjoys the wildness in the Florida landscape every chance he gets.

HARRIET BEECHER STOWE (1811–1896) wrote more than thirty books and is best known for her internationally acclaimed 1852 novel *Uncle Tom's Cabin,* which roused anti-slavery sentiments in the United States. After the Civil War, Stowe and her family wintered for many years in Mandarin, Florida, where she promoted the state in articles describing the area's natural beauty. Her essay in this collection appeared in 1873 in the *Christian Union* newspaper.

CLAIRE STROM is the Rapetti-Trunzo Chair of History at Rollins College. She has published widely in the history of public health, the American South, and agriculture. She loves living in Florida and is an avid kayaker.

TERRY ANN THAXTON, a fifth-generation Floridian, has published three books of poems: *Getaway Girl; The Terrible Wife,* which won a Florida Book

Awards bronze medal; and *Mud Song*, which won the T. S. Eliot 2017 Poetry Prize and a Florida Book Awards silver medal. She teaches creative writing at the University of Central Florida in Orlando.

MARGARET ROSS TOLBERT is a Gainesville-based artist whose work is an effect of immersion in water, especially from the springs heartland of the Floridan aquifer. Her paintings have been in installations and collections on four continents, and she uses them to connect viewers to water as subject, cultural traditions in water, and the water's point of view.

MARK JEROME WALTERS is a professor of journalism and digital communication at the University of South Florida St. Petersburg. He has a BA in English literature from McGill University, an MA from the Columbia University School of Journalism, and a DVM in international veterinary medicine from Tufts University. He has written six books. His most recent is about the imperiled Florida scrub-jay.

PATSY WEST is an author and ethno-historian. For the past forty years she has collaborated with the Seminole and Miccosukee people for publications and projects encompassing some 250 years of tribal history, culture, and art.

Credits

Unless noted below, all essays and poems are appearing in print for the first time.

"Some Days the Sea" from *Looking for The Gulf Motel* by Richard Blanco, 2012. Reprinted by permission of the University of Pittsburgh Press.

Excerpt from *A Seminole Legend: The Life and Times of Betty Mae Jumper*, by Betty Mae Tiger Jumper and Patsy West, 2001. Reprinted by permission of the University Press of Florida.

"The Habits of Alligators" from *Totch: A Life in the Everglades*, by Loren G. "Totch" Brown, 1993. Reprinted by permission of the University Press of Florida.

"Innocence Found" from *Maximum Insight: Selected Columns by Bill Maxwell*, by Bill Maxwell, 2001. Reprinted by permission of the University Press of Florida.

"Our Land" reproduced from *Buffalo Tiger: A Life in the Everglades* by Buffalo Tiger and Harry A. Kersey Jr., 2002. Used by permission of the University of Nebraska Press.

"One Manatee, Two Nations" by Anmari Alvarez Aleman, derived from an op-ed published December 31, 2015, in the *Tampa Bay Times*. Used with permission.

Excerpts from "the Galley" published by the *Miami Herald*, various dates, 1920–1922.

"Up the Okalawaha—A Sail into Fairy-Land" by Mrs. H. B. Stowe. Originally published in *Christian Union* (1870–1893); May 14, 1873.

"Biscayne National Monument: Preserving Our Precious Bays" by Nathaniel Pryor Reed originally appeared in a lengthier form in *Travels on the Green Highway: An Environmentalist's Journey*. Hobe Sound, Florida: Reed Publishing Company LLC, 2016. Used with permission.